A TASTE OF THE

Mediterranean

VEGETARIAN STYLE

"Enjoy"

Mary Salloum

Egypt

France

Greece

Italy

Lebanon

Morocco

Spain

Turkey

D0796732

by **Mary Salloum**

Photographed on the front cover

Top Left — Ratatouille (France), page 126
Top Right — Vegetarian Paella (Spain), page 119
Bottom Left — Falafel (Lebanon), page 112
Bottom Right — Insalata Caprese (Italy), page 39

A Taste of the Mediterranean
by Mary Salloum

Published by A Taste of Lebanon Enterprises
Second Printing, July 2000

Copyright © 1993 by
A Taste of Lebanon Enterprises
P.O. Box 6110, Stn. "A"
Calgary, Alberta, Canada T2H 2L4

Canadian Cataloguing in Publication Data

Salloum, Mary, 1943-

A taste of the Mediterranean — vegetarian style

Includes index.
ISBN 1-895292-17-4

1. Cookery, Mediterranean.   2. Vegetarian cookery.
I. Title

TX725.M35S24 1992   641.59'1638   C 92-098192-5

Food Photography by Ross (Hutch) Hutchinson
Hutchinson and Company, Calgary, Alberta

Back Cover Photo by Coates Photographics
Calgary, Alberta

Dishes and Accessories Courtesy of:
Shakeh Dayal, Shakeh's Kitchen
Benkris & Co., Mount Royal Village
Bistro La Moda
Calgary, Alberta

Designed, Printed and Produced in Canada by:
Centax Books, a Division of PrintWest Communications Ltd.
Publishing Director, Photo Designer & Food Stylist: Margo Embury
1150 Eighth Avenue, Regina, Saskatchewan, Canada S4R 1C9
(306) 525-2304   FAX (306) 757-2439
E-mail: centax@printwest.com www.centaxbooks.com

WITH LOVE TO

DANIEL

AND

DANA

ACKNOWLEDGEMENTS

My sincere thanks to Patricia Van Heerden, a good customer and vegetarian, for encouraging me to write a vegetarian cookbook.

Special thanks to my family and friends, especially Amy, Myles and Donna, for tasting and testing these vegetarian recipes.

My grateful appreciation to my friend, Shakeh Dayal, for allowing me to borrow from her wonderful collection of dishes and linens for the food photography.

My gratitude to Margo Embury for her expert assistance in food styling and editing.

TABLE OF CONTENTS

FROM THE AUTHOR

The thought of food makes us happy. It puts a smile on our faces. It enhances romantic times with that special someone. It spices up conversation with friends and provides an exchange of traditions and cultures. Above all, it unites families at mealtime.

When I published my first cookbook, *A Taste of Lebanon,* in 1983, I had no idea that vegetarian food was so popular. Then, in 1985, along with my son, Daniel, and daughter, Dana, I opened the Cedars Restaurant and Deli in downtown Calgary. We were forced almost immediately into expansion as the lunch crowds kept growing and growing. Falafel suddenly became the best-selling sandwich. The Cedars Falafel Hut evolved two years later at the university where the exotic flavors of the Lebanese fare attracted the trendsetting generation. Although we offer a wide selection of meatless dishes on our menu, I am constantly besieged to include even more.

I have wonderful, happy memories of my own mother's fantastic cooking and the delicious aromas that would drift from her busy kitchen. I will always remember coming home from school and being greeted by the scent of freshly baked bread and other delectable treats as I walked up the sidewalk. To this day, when my sister, brothers and I visit our parent's home, that same old feeling returns. Even if we've just finished a meal before arriving, we are easily enticed by the delicious feast she prepares in no time.

I was nine years old when my family came to Canada from Lebanon. I've always loved and appreciated the culture and traditions of my native country. Sharing the Lebanese cuisine with others has been my passion for the past decade. I've been thrilled to find that people from all nationalities and walks of life love this food.

I have thoroughly enjoyed researching and tasting recipes from other countries around the Mediterranean in the creation of this book. Blending such exciting flavors, scents and presentations has been a rewarding experience for me. I hope you will value and share this culinary collection with your family and friends. Now prepare yourself for a tantalizing journey through the beautiful countries of the Mediterranean.

Mary Salloum

Mary Salloum

MAP OF THE
MEDITERRANEAN AREA

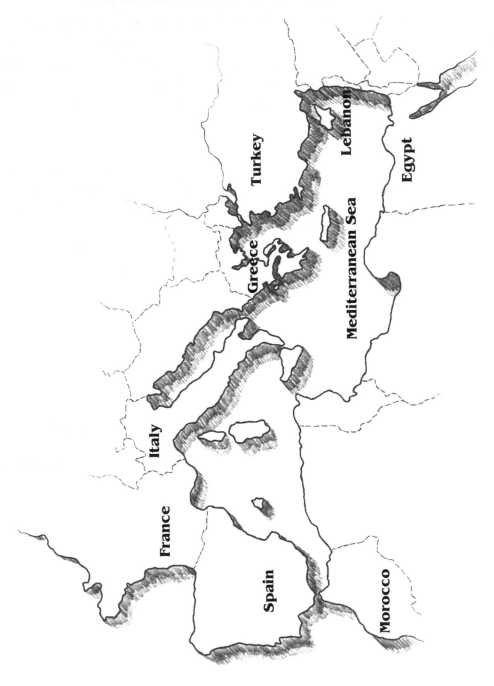

INTRODUCTION

Today, people everywhere are conscious of what is good for them. They are choosing foods that are natural and healthy. People have enjoyed meatless meals for centuries, and now many are returning to the basics.

You don't have to be a vegetarian to enjoy these recipes. *A Taste of the Mediterranean* provides an amazing selection of meatless dishes for everyone; many are exciting enough to be served as a main course.

In the following pages you will be introduced to a delicious variety of soups, salads, appetizers, main courses, side dishes and desserts. This cookbook is an invaluable source of information, and contains step-by-step directions to guide you easily through the recipes.

Many people say it's a healthy way of eating. Some say it's an inexpensive way to cook. Others want to avoid meat for environmental, humanitarian or religious purposes. Whether it's a health conscious decision or the desire to try something new, vegetarian cooking is adventurous, nutritious and delicious. You will find these dishes filling and satisfying.

As we visit each country we will be collecting a culinary treasury of appetizing and exotic meals. *A Taste of the Mediterranean* will guide you on a culinary discovery trip around the Mediterranean with vegetables, beans, grains, herbs and spices being featured. Whether grilled, broiled, sautéed, braised, baked, boiled or roasted, they are always delicious.

These ingredients are reaching stardom and are fast becoming fashionable foods. The precious gift from the Gods, "olive oil," has made its presence felt in today's market. This staple ingredient is a monounsaturated oil that helps to lower blood LDL (bad) cholesterol and maintain good levels of HDL (beneficial) cholesterol.

This culinary adventure affords us the opportunity to experience the superb cuisine of France. Then on to Italy to savor the flavor and aroma of some of the best-loved and known foods of the world. In Greece, we sample the classical heritage of food from the cradle of Mediterranean and Western civilization. In Lebanon, we linger for an exciting and distinctive menu, sampling the exotic flavors of the Middle East. When we travel further, we are tempted by the colorful culinary creativity of Spain. As we journey back into Morocco, Egypt and Turkey, we realize that the foods of the world overlap, each borrowing from the other and providing enrichment to all. Similarities in the ingredients are very evident in the Mediterranean countries, but the preparation differs greatly. They each utilize their skill and imagination to produce their own unique cuisines.

Now you can indulge in the Mediterranean's finest dishes, completing your own menu by borrowing a little from each country and using creativity and imagination to produce elegant, nutritious meals from *A Taste of the Mediterranean*.

SPICES AND HERBS

Allspice — Dark reddish brown berries similar to a large peppercorn in size. Flavor is like a combination of cloves, cinammon and nutmeg. Very popular in the Middle East. Often used in baking, stews and to flavor rice.

Bay Leaf — Shiny, leathery green leaves of a small shrub or tree. Widely grown in the Mediterranean. Strongly aromatic, used in almost every cuisine in the world, but especially in French cooking. Essential for use in stocks, soups, sauces, marinades, as well as pickles and brines.

Basil — Often called Sweet Basil is very much associated with the Mediterranean cooking of the south of France and Italy. Available fresh or dried. Strong, sweet-scented perfume. It is one of the most alluring herbs. Its distinctive flavor transforms simple vegetables into exotic dishes. It freezes well, but is best preserved with oil in the Italian manner.

Cayenne — Blended finely ground powder of the dried fruit of pungent varieties of red chili. Pod-like fruits are usually small, slender, green and yellow, when mature and ripe they turn red. Beware of this one, very hot. Flavors soups, chilies, stews and curries.

Chili peppers — Berry-like fruits with a shiny outer skin. They vary in size, shape, color and pungency. Ranging from green when unripe to red, yellow, brown and purplish-black; from tiny to extremely large, and from mild to very hot. Remedies are milk, yogurt or ice cream. Used in French sauces, Spanish cuisine and throughout the Mediterranean.

Coriander — (Cilantro) also called Chinese parsley, native to the Middle East and Southern Europe, but grown world wide. Seeds are available whole or ground. Use fresh leaves, whole or chopped, in salads, stuffings or stews.

Cumin — Native to the Eastern Mediterranean and upper Egypt. Grows well in hot countries. Small dried seeds similar to caraway. Available whole or ground. Use in bulgar (crushed wheat), vegetable, and especially eggplant dishes.

Dill — Used widely by Egyptians and Greeks and throughout Southern Europe. Available in seed form or fresh. Use in pickling vegetables, add to soups and stocks, pastries, stuffings and yogurt and sour cream dishes.

Fennel — Feathery leaves grown on stalks, used as a herb. Suitable for drying. Seeds available whole or ground. Grown in the Mediterranean countries and now grown world wide. Use in soups and sauces, for flavoring breads and cakes.

Garlic — Bulb of the lily plant, consisting of several cloves. Grown world wide, a native of Asia. Claims to have many medicinal purposes, including remarkable abilities to destroy disease and infection. Fresh is best. Garlic powder looses flavor and aroma (see helpful hints). Use in salads, soups, sauces and most Mediterranean cooking.

Ginger — Bulbous-knobbed root, hot spicy flavor. Available fresh or dried. Native of South-East Asia, but has now worked its way over to the Mediterranean and throughout the world. An excellent addition to pickles, chutney, cakes, puddings and vegetable dishes.

Mint — Has been flavoring foods since the beginning of time. It is an ancient Greek symbol of hospitality. One common mint is peppermint. Very aromatic and peppery in flavor, it is hot but refreshing. Spearmint has a milder flavor and aroma. Mint is much used throughout the Mediterranean. Does not combine well with some other herbs. Very common in the Middle East, where it is used in salads, mint tea, yogurt-based soups and sauces. It is used often in French and Italian cuisines, in mint jelly, potatoes and peas.

Oregano — Aromatic, perennial plant grown in the Mediterranean and Asia. Leaves are hardy, flavor is peppery and has a slightly bitter tang. Use fresh or dried with care as this herb is strong. Use in all vegetable dishes, especially zucchini, soups, salads, bean dishes and stews.

Parsley — This is one of the oldest, longest known herbs, very widely used, fresh or dried, all over the world. It dates back to Greece and was well known in Britain and France in Medieval times. Curly type is most popular in Britain and Northern America. Flat-leaved parsley is better known in Europe and throughout the Mediterranean. Used to flavor salads, essential in making Tabouli Salad (page 40), soups, stocks, stews, dressings and vegetable dishes.

Rosemary — A Mediterranean plant, rosemary means "Dew of the Sea". It thrives on Mediterranean hillsides. Leaves resemble pine needles, has a powerful, faintly pine-like aroma with a strong earth taste. Used fresh or dried. Used widely in Italy. Good with vegetables and often used with garlic.

Saffron — Grown throughout the Mediterranean, Spain, Turkey, Iran and China. Native of South-East Asia and Greece. The Queen of Spices, rare and very precious, a powder made from stigmas of Autumn Crocus Blossoms. Golden color, pleasant flavor, available in powder form or thread-like strands. Flavors rice, cakes, pastries, puddings. It's "worth its weight in gold."

Sesame Seeds — Tiny flat seeds, used whole or ground into a paste, Tahini. An annual, it is a native of India, now widely grown in China, the Middle East, Africa, Mexico and Texas, U.S.A. May be used toasted or fresh. Very common ingredient in a Middle Eastern home and throughout the Mediterranean. A main ingredient for making Hommous (page 23). Use seeds when making breads, cookies, cakes, halva or to sprinkle on salads.

Tarragon — A distinctive culinary herb. Widely used in French Cuisine. Has a delicate flavor, unlike any other, remarkably powerful. French Tarragon is a long thinned-leaved variety. The Russian has broader leaves and a less-pleasant flavor. Freezes and dries well. Used sparingly in omelettes, sauces, eggs, salads and stuffings.

Thyme — Garden Thyme is the most common of the many varieties of this mint-related herb. It dates back to classical Greece. Another pungent herb, admired for its flavorful leaves. Freezes and dries well. Use in stuffings, salads, vegetables, stews, add to marinated olives.

Turmeric — Belongs to the Ginger family. Roots are ground. Yellow-orange in color. An agreeable aroma, warm and spicy taste. Native of South-Eastern Asia. It flavors and colors all types of dishes such as rice, bulgar, vegetables, pickles and sweets. Often used as an economical coloring substitute for saffron.

HELPFUL HINTS

Beans and Peas — Soak dried beans and peas overnight. Drain and freeze in plastic bags. Take out what is required for a recipe.

Bulgar — (crushed wheat) is wheat that has been cooked, then dried and separated into 2 sizes. **Fine** which is used for everything. **Coarse** is used for pilaf dishes. Make sure that the bulgar is not cracked wheat, this has not been cooked first.

Citrus fruits — To get more juice out of them, heat in an oven for a few minutes or immerse in boiling water for 5 minutes or press firmly on the fruit and roll it with the palm of your hand to soften.

Eggs — Soak egg-covered utensils in cold water (hot water sets the egg) then wash in hot water.

Garlic — To have garlic ready for use in a recipe, put the peeled garlic bulbs in oil in a small jar with a tight-fitting lid. Keeps for weeks refrigerated. The oil can be used in your salad dressings.

Herbs and Spices — Keep on hand: cinnamon, nutmeg, thyme, bay leaves, parsley, cloves, marjoram, tarragon, garlic, onion, oregano, basil, saffron, turmeric, coriander, cumin, ground ginger, fresh ginger (will keep for months if refrigerated, peel and cover in dry sherry in a jar with a tight-fitting lid), cayenne, black and white pepper, salt.

Note: ½ tsp. (2 mL) of crushed dried herbs equals 1 tbsp. (15 mL) of chopped fresh herbs.

Use herbs and spices a little at a time. If too little is used, you can always add more at any time. Some have strong flavors; these include rosemary, sage, dill, tarragon and mint.

Herbs can be dried or frozen when in season and used in the winter months.

Nuts — Use a blender or food processor to chop nuts and seeds.

Tomatoes — Freeze well. No need to blanch. Place in airtight containers. Excellent to use in soups, casseroles and for sauces. To peel plunge into boiling water for 15-20 seconds, then into ice-cold water.

Vegetables — When peeling vegetables, remove as thin a layer of skin as possible. Vegetables in their skins retain more food value.

Do not cut vegetables into too small pieces for cooking. If left in larger pieces there will be less nutrient loss.

All frozen vegetables (except corn on the cob) should be cooked without thawing. Use only a small amount of water and cover tightly to bring to a boil.

Yogurt — Gives extra lightness to an omelette. Use 1 tbsp. (15 mL) for every 2 eggs. Beat well and cook as usual. Try this for scrambled eggs also. Yogurt contains B vitamins, calcium and protein. It provides the digestive system with good bacteria.

Appetizers
and
Sauces

Sangria

Serve this colorful drink from southern Spain with a variety of tapas or appetizers.

1 cup	water	250 mL
½ cup	sugar	125 mL
¾ cup	light corn syrup	175 mL
1	orange, sliced	1
1	lemon, sliced	1
1	lime, sliced	1
26 oz.	bottle inexpensive red wine	750 mL
3 cups	club soda	750 mL
	ice cubes	

Boil the water and sugar together in a large saucepan for 10 minutes. Cool.

In a 2-quart (2 L) pitcher, combine all ingredients. Stir and add ice cubes.

Green and Red Pepper Tapas

A tapas delicacy to add to your collection.

2	large green peppers	2
2	large red or orange peppers	2
¼ cup	olive oil	60 mL
6	garlic cloves, peeled and sliced	6

Set oven at 400°F (200°C).

Roast the peppers on a baking sheet for 15 minutes. Turn them over and bake for 10 minutes more. Remove from oven and wrap each one in a paper towel or place them in a paper bag. Set aside to cool.

Peel the skin from the peppers and remove seeds. Slice peppers into ¼" (1 cm) strips.

Heat oil in frying pan on low heat, add garlic. When garlic is golden brown, add the pepper strips.

Sauté for 5-7 minutes, shaking the pan occasionally.

Serve warm or cold.

See photograph on page 122.

Escalibada

Grilled Vegetables

These are best cooked on the barbecue, but can be cooked under the broiler.

2	red peppers	2
2	green peppers	2
2	medium eggplants	2
4	medium tomatoes	4

DRESSING

1 tbsp.	chopped parsley	15 mL
¼ cup	olive oil	60 mL
2 tbsp.	vinegar	30 mL
1	garlic clove, minced	1

Grill the peppers over moderate heat on the barbecue. Pierce the skin of the eggplants so they do not burst when extremely hot. Grill the eggplants with the peppers for 15-20 minutes, turning several times. The peppers will cook faster than the eggplants. When skins become charred and blistered, remove from heat. Wrap eggplant and peppers in paper towel or place in a paper bag. Set aside.

Score the skin of the tomatoes by making a cross cutting on the skin and grill for 5 minutes, turning at regular intervals.

Peel skin off the peppers and remove seeds. Peel eggplants and tomatoes. Slice all vegetables. Mix all dressing ingredients together.

Arrange vegetables on a serving platter with sliced tomatoes in the center. Drizzle dressing over all the vegetables.

Serve hot or cold as a side dish, as a meal with bread or with Ali-oli (page 18).

Try this dish along with other tapas.

NOTE:
Wrapping or covering the peppers and eggplants makes them easier to peel.

See photograph on page 122.

Ali-oli

Garlic Sauce

This is a very popular Spanish garlic sauce. It is served with many dishes including Paella, Escalibada and any vegetable dish.

3	garlic cloves, minced	3
	salt to taste	
2	egg yolks	2
1 cup	olive oil	250 mL
1 tbsp.	lemon juice	15 mL

All ingredients should be at room temperature.

Place garlic, salt and egg yolks in blender or food processor; whip and gradually add the oil, a drop at a time at first, beating constantly. Add a little of the lemon juice from time to time. When sauce begins to thicken, add the remainder of the oil in a thin stream.

Pour into a serving bowl.

Kmaj Mahamas

Pita Chips

A wonderful snack for dipping.

4	7" (18 cm) pita bread rounds	4
¼ cup	olive oil	60 mL
2	garlic cloves, minced or	2
	1 tsp. (5 mL) garlic powder	
½ tsp.	oregano	2 mL
½ tsp.	thyme	2 mL

Set oven at 350°F (190°C).

Open pita around the edges to make 8 rounds. Mix oil and garlic together. Brush oil mixture over each round. Stack all the rounds. Cut through all the layers, making 8 wedges. Sprinkle with remaining herbs. Toss well. Place on a baking sheet in a single layer.

Bake in center of oven for 10 minutes, or until crisp and golden brown.

May be served with Hommous (page 23) or Tahini sauce (page 23).

See photograph on page 87.

Spanakopita

Spinach with Fyllo

Makes 8

This delicate hors d'oeuvre is filled with cheese and spinach. Absolutely delicious and very popular, it is served hot or cold.

½ cup	melted unsalted butter, first amount	125 mL
6	green onions, chopped	6
1	large bunch spinach, cleaned and chopped	1
3 tbsp.	chopped fresh dill or 1½ tsp. (7 mL) dry	45 mL
4	eggs, lightly beaten	4
1 cup	crumbled feta cheese	250 mL
1 cup	ricotta cheese	250 mL
½ tsp.	nutmeg	2 mL
1 lb.	fyllo pastry sheets at room temperature	454 g
½ cup	melted unsalted butter, second amount	125 mL

Heat butter in a medium-sized saucepan on medium heat. Add the green onions, stirring until soft. Add spinach and dill, cook and stir for 3 minutes, or until spinach wilts; cool.

Squeeze excess liquid from spinach mixture. Place the spinach in a mixing bowl. Add eggs, cheeses and nutmeg. Mix well.

Set oven at 350°F (180°C).

Brush 2 sheets of fyllo lightly with melted butter. Place them on top of each other. Cut pastry widthwise into 8 strips. Place 1 tbsp. (15 mL) of the mixture at one end of each strip; fold over the end to cover the filling. To shape a triangle, fold the end corner diagonally across to the other edge to form a triangle. Continue folding over, left then right to the end of strip, making sure to keep the triangular shape. Repeat procedure until all strips are used. Place triangles on ungreased baking sheet and brush tops and sides with butter.

Bake for 20-25 minutes, or until golden brown.

Bruschetta con Pomodoro

Italy

Bruschetta with Tomatoes

Serves 8

A popular appetizer served in many Italian restaurants in North America.

3	large tomatoes, finely chopped	3
¼ cup	olive oil	60 mL
½ cup	finely chopped fresh basil	125 mL
	salt and freshly ground pepper to taste	
8	¾″ (2 cm) thick slices Italian or French bread	8
3	garlic cloves, minced	3

Preheat broiler. Toss the first 3 ingredients in a mixing bowl. Season with salt and pepper.

Place bread on baking sheet and broil until light brown, turn over and brown the other side.

Rub garlic into the toasted bread. Mound the tomato mixture on top.

Serve on a platter.

VARIATION:
Add finely chopped green peppers and onions to tomato mixture.

See photograph on page 70.

Baked Brie

France

Serves 8-10

This is an elegant entrée served with a salad, sliced French bread, grapes or other fruits and a bottle of white wine. Serve Brie and fruit as an appetizer for a large gathering.

¼ cup	butter, softened	60 mL
1½ lb.	wheel of Brie cheese with rind	750 g
½ cup	sliced almonds	125 mL

Heat oven to 350°F (180°C).

Spread butter over top and sides of the cheese. Place on an ovenproof serving platter. Sprinkle almonds over top.

Bake for 35-40 minutes, or until cheese begins to melt.

Serve warm with sliced bread or crackers.

VARIATION:
(1) Use 7 oz. (200g) Brie, 2 tbsp. (30 mL) butter and 2 tbsp. (30 mL) sliced almonds for topping.
(2) Spread 1 cup (250 mL) cooked whole cranberries over the top, serve as is without baking.

Fried Olives

Serve these fried olives with other tapas dishes.

1½ cups	green olives with pits	375 mL
2	eggs, beaten	2
4 tbsp.	flour	60 mL
2 cups	olive oil	500 mL

Coat the olives with beaten egg, then roll them in the flour. Coat very well. Heat oil on medium heat. Fry olives until golden brown.

Serve warm on a bed of shredded lettuce.

See photograph on page 122.

Flori di Zucchine Fritti

Zucchini Blossom Fritters

For those who grow zucchini, try this very popular recipe using the blossoms.

20	zucchini blossoms	20
1½ cups	flour	375 mL
¾ cup	milk	175 mL
4	eggs, beaten	4
	cooking oil	
	salt	

Open the blossoms and remove the pistils. Wash blossoms gently without damaging them and lay them on a cloth to dry.

Combine flour and milk until smooth. Add beaten eggs, stir well.

In a frying pan, heat ½" (1.3 cm) oil to 375°F (190°C).

Coat each blossom in the batter, shake gently to allow excess batter to drip off.

Fry a few blossoms at a time until golden brown, turning until all sides are crisp. Remove with a slotted spoon and drain on absorbent paper. Sprinkle with salt while still hot.

Arrange on a serving platter. Serve immediately.

Toasted Almonds

A tasty snack, for tapas.

4 tbsp.	olive or vegetable oil	60 mL
1½ cups	blanched almonds	375 mL
¼ tsp.	cumin	1 mL
	salt	

Warm the oil in a heavy skillet; add the almonds and sauté on low to medium heat until golden brown. Drain on paper towels. Sprinkle with cumin and a pinch of salt.

Raisins or dried fruit pieces may be added.

See photograph on page 122.

Louse Ma Thoom

Almond Pâté

This marvellous recipe was given to me by Renée. She uses it when entertaining.

1 cup	blanched almonds, toasted	250 mL
3	garlic cloves	3
1	medium onion, coarsely chopped	1
2 tbsp.	butter or olive oil	30 mL
12 oz.	mushrooms, halved	340 g
½ tsp.	salt	2 mL
½ tsp.	pepper	2 mL
½ tsp.	thyme	2 mL

Chop almonds in food processor until very fine.

In a large frying pan, sauté garlic and onion in the butter until onions are tender. Add all remaining ingredients. Sauté for approximately 5 minutes, until mushrooms are limp.

Add this mixture to the chopped almonds. Chop well to achieve a paste.

Place in a shallow dish and surround with crackers, melba toast, pita chips or French bread slices.

Hommous bi Tahini

Hommous

Lebanon

Serves 4

This dip, with its delightful tangy flavor, is the most popular Middle Eastern dip.

19 oz.	can chickpeas or garbanzo beans, drained	540 mL
¼ cup	tahini (sesame seed paste)	60 mL
1-2	garlic cloves	1-2
½ tsp.	salt	2 mL
¼ cup	lemon juice or to taste	60 mL

Combine all ingredients in a food processor or blender. Blend for 2-3 minutes to a smooth paste. Blend in a little water if a thinner dip is preferred. Place in a small platter or shallow bowl. If desired, sprinkle olive oil on top and garnish with parsley sprigs, lemon wedges and green onions.

To serve, tear off pieces of pita bread or cut pita into wedges and dip into Hommous or use as a dip for raw vegetables.

Serve with Tabouli (page 40).

Tahini-Taratour

Sesame Seed Sauce

Lebanon

Makes 1 cup (250 mL)

The most versatile of all sauces in the Middle East, this is the main ingredient for making Hommous. Tangy, tasty and tantalizing.

1	garlic clove	1
½ tsp.	salt	2 mL
⅓ cup	tahini (sesame seed paste)	75 mL
⅓ cup	lemon juice	75 mL
½ cup	cold water	125 mL

Chop garlic in food processor or blender. Add salt. Before measuring, stir the tahini in the jar. Place all remaining ingredients in the processor; blend until smooth, scraping sides of bowl at intervals. Serve as a dip or dressing for raw or cooked vegetables or pita wedges.

NOTE:
For thinner or thicker sauce adjust the water to suit your taste.

Labani

Yogurt Cheese

This is a staple in every Lebanese home.

1 qt.	**plain yogurt**	**1 L**
1 tsp.	**salt**	**5 mL**

Pour the cold yogurt into a cloth or cheesecloth bag doubled in thickness and tied. Hang and let drain for 1 day, at room temperature, placing a pan underneath to catch the drippings.

Remove yogurt from bag and place in a mixing bowl. Add salt and mix well. Refrigerate in a suitable covered container.

To serve, a sprinkle of olive oil may be spread over the yogurt or spread yogurt on pita bread, add a sprinkle of olive oil and dry mint and place under the broiler for 2 minutes.

Serve for breakfast, for a snack with olives, or spread on toast.

NOTE:
If only a small amount of yogurt cheese is to be made, place fresh cold yogurt in a coffee filter and let drain into a container.

Tzatziki

Yogurt Cucumber Dip

This is delicious served with kabobs or as a dip for vegetables or pita.

1	**long English cucumber**	**1**
3	**garlic cloves, minced**	**3**
2½ tsp.	**salt**	**12 mL**
2 cups	**yogurt**	**500 mL**
1 cup	**sour cream**	**250 mL**
1 tsp.	**chopped parsley**	**5 mL**

Grate cucumber into a bowl. Set aside to allow the liquid to drain off.

Place garlic and salt in a serving bowl, add yogurt and sour cream. Squeeze out excess liquid from cucumber. Add cucumber to yogurt mixture. Mix well. Sprinkle with parsley.

See photograph on page 52.

Turkish Eggplant Salad

Turkey

Serves 6

1	large eggplant, about 1½ lbs. (750 g)	1
2 tbsp.	olive oil	30 mL
2 tbsp.	lemon juice	30 mL
1	garlic clove, minced	1
1	medium green pepper, seeded and finely chopped	1
1 cup	plain yogurt	250 mL
½ tsp.	salt or to taste	2 mL
¼ tsp.	pepper or to taste	1 mL
	romaine lettuce (use only the inside leaves)	
3	tomatoes, cut in wedges	3
1	small red onion, sliced into rings	1
2 tbsp.	chopped parsley	30 mL

Set oven at 400°F (200°C).

Pierce eggplant skin with a fork. Place eggplant in a pan. Bake for 1 hour or until very soft. Cool and cut in half. Scoop out pulp, place in a bowl and mash with a fork. Mix in oil, lemon juice, garlic, green pepper, yogurt, salt and pepper. Cover and chill.

Arrange romaine lettuce on individual salad plates. Mound eggplant in the center of each leaf. Surround salad with tomato wedges and top with onion rings and parsley.

Serve with pieces of pita bread.

VARIATION:
Sour cream may be substituted for plain yogurt.

See photograph on page 156.

Moroccan Shredded Carrots

Morocco

Serves 4

This recipe is delicious served with barbecued vegetables.

2	large carrots, shredded	2
¼ cup	olive oil or to taste	60 mL
3 tbsp.	lemon juice	45 mL
2	garlic cloves, minced	2
	salt and pepper to taste	

Scrape, then shred carrots. Place in a small mixing bowl and add all remaining ingredients. Cover and refrigerate until chilled.

Serve as an appetizer or side dish.

Turkish Fava Bean Salad

Fava beans or broad beans are frequently used in Mediterranean cooking. This recipe is more like a spread than a salad.

1½ cups	dried fava beans, soaked overnight	375 mL
1	large onion, quartered	1
2 qts.	cold water	2 L
1 tsp.	sugar	5 mL
	salt and pepper to taste	
6 tbsp.	lemon juice	90 mL
6 tbsp.	olive oil	90 mL
1 tbsp.	sour cream	15 mL
1 cup	chopped green onions	250 mL
2 tbsp.	chopped fresh dill or ½ tsp. (2 mL) dry	30 mL
2 tbsp.	chopped parsley	30 mL
6	black olives	6
6	radishes, cut into roses, for garnish	6

Drain the beans and rinse well. Place them in a large saucepan with the onion and water. Bring to a boil. Simmer and stir frequently until tender, approximately 45 minutes to 1 hour. Add more water if required. When beans are done, most of the water will have evaporated.

When beans are tender, remove from heat. Mash with potato masher or food processor. They should be the consistency of thick mashed potatoes.

Add sugar, salt and pepper, 2 tbsp. (30 mL) of lemon juice, 2 tbsp. (30 mL) of oil and the sour cream.

Spoon the mixture onto a small platter and spread not quite to the edges. Cool. Garnish with the chopped green onions, dill, parsley, olives and radish roses.

Blend together the remaining lemon juice and oil. Add salt to taste and serve separately.

Serve as a side dish or appetizer with pita bread pieces.

Salads

Salade d'Aubergines et d'Oranges

Eggplant and Orange Salad

France

Serves 4-6

A delicious accompaniment to any meal.

2	**medium eggplants, peeled and cut into 1" (2.5 cm) cubes**	2
¼ **cup**	**salt**	60 mL
⅓ **cup**	**olive oil**	75 mL
¾ **cup**	**finely chopped green onions**	175 mL
2	**garlic cloves, crushed**	2
1 **tbsp.**	**grated orange rind**	15 mL
¼ **cup**	**white wine vinegar**	60 mL
	salt and pepper to taste	
	orange segments for garnish	
	fresh mint leaves for garnish	

Place eggplant in a colander and sprinkle with salt. Leave to drain for 30 minutes. Rinse and pat dry with paper towels. Sprinkle with pepper. Heat ½ of the oil in a large skillet. Fry the onions on medium heat for 3 minutes. Add the garlic, sauté for 2 more minutes. Add remaining oil, then the eggplant. Fry on medium heat for 3-4 minutes. Add orange rind, vinegar, salt and pepper. Simmer until eggplant is tender, approximately 15 minutes, stirring occasionally. Cool then chill.

Serve in center of serving plates. Garnish with a border of orange segments and fresh mint leaves.

See photograph on page 34.

Moroccan Orange Salad with Olives

This is a very dramatic looking dish and very refreshing with the sliced oranges.

2 cups	shredded lettuce	500 mL
2	large oranges, peeled and thinly sliced	2
1	large onion, thinly sliced	1
10	black olives, sliced	10
¼ tsp.	salt	1 mL
	dash of cayenne pepper	
2 tbsp.	olive oil	30 mL
2 tbsp.	lemon juice	30 mL

On a platter, place the shredded lettuce and arrange the orange slices over the lettuce. Top with the sliced onions and the olives. Combine all remaining ingredients and blend well. Drizzle oil mixture on top of the salad.

Cacik

Turkish Cucumber Salad

There are many variations of this refreshing cucumber and mint salad throughout the Mediterranean.

1 cup	plain yogurt	250 mL
2 tbsp.	chopped fresh mint or ½ tsp. (2 mL) dry	30 mL
1 tbsp.	lemon juice	15 mL
1	garlic clove, minced	1
	dash of pepper	
1	medium long English cucumber, unpeeled, thinly sliced	1
	mint leaves	

Combine all ingredients, except cucumber and mint leaves, in a mixing bowl. Cover and refrigerate.

Just before serving, stir in the cucumber.

Place in a serving dish and garnish with the mint leaves.

Salatat Khodra

Layered Salad

Serves 6

This salad not only tastes great, but it is visually beautiful. The dressing is a classic Lebanese salad dressing.

2	medium-sized zucchini	2
2	large tomatoes	2
2	long English cucumbers	2
1	medium purple onion	1
2	large red peppers	2
8	romaine lettuce leaves	8
	Classic Lebanese Dressing (recipe below)	

Thinly slice first 4 ingredients, dice peppers, tear lettuce into bite-sized pieces.

Layer all the vegetables in a large clear glass bowl alternating color and variety. Make sure the vegetables reach the sides of the bowl so each layer is visible through the glass. Drizzle dressing over all (recipe follows). If not serving salad immediately, prepare dressing and drizzle on top at time of serving.

CLASSIC LEBANESE DRESSING

This dressing can be used for any salad or for marinated beans.

¼ cup	lemon juice	60 mL
2	garlic cloves, minced	2
¼ cup	olive oil	60 mL
½ tsp.	salt	2 mL
¼ tsp.	pepper	1 mL
¼ cup	finely chopped fresh mint or 2 tbsp. (30 mL) dry	60 mL

Mix all ingredients together in a small bowl.

See photograph on page 87.

Xato

Catalonian salad with peppery sauce. What a way to use that chicory in the garden! This is the vegetarian version.

	Garlic Almond Dressing (recipe below)	
1	**head chicory or endive**	1
1	**long English cucumber, thinly sliced**	1
1	**large tomato, cubed**	1

Prepare dressing.

Tear the chicory or endive into bite-sized pieces, place in a salad bowl. Add the cucumber and tomato. Add dressing, toss gently and serve.

GARLIC ALMOND DRESSING

4	**garlic cloves**	4
12	**blanched almonds, toasted**	12
1	**small chili pepper, seeded and chopped or**	1
	¼ tsp. (1 mL) dry cayenne pepper	
¼ cup	**olive oil**	60 mL
2 tbsp.	**wine vinegar**	30 mL
½ tsp.	**salt**	2 mL

Crush the garlic and almonds in blender, food processor or use a pestle and mortar. Add the chili pepper and blend thoroughly. Gradually blend in the oil, then vinegar and salt.

France

France is almost self sufficient in agriculture. For such a small country, it is richer in foodstuffs than any other nation. The richest agricultural districts lie in the north, where wheat is a staple crop. Fruit is plentiful and grows abundantly in the south.

The French make use of everything edible and cooking is treated as a fine art. In the south of France the cooking is oil-based and in the north it is butter-based. The French have a passion for quality and always strive to prepare each dish to perfection. There is some evidence of Spanish influence in the south of France. For instance, there are similarities in the combination of tomatoes, peppers and eggs when preparing Pepper and Tomato Omelette (page 106).

Herbs are a necessity. Basil is exported into the United States, Hungary and Belgium. The French somehow achieve the most delectable flavor from their ingredients by using rosemary, summer savory, thyme, tarragon and garlic to enhance their consummate cuisine.

The day usually begins with a simple breakfast of cheese, fruit, croissants and omelettes. At noon, a 4-or 5-course meal begins with hors d'oeuvres which are eaten at the table with a knife and fork. These could include cooked or raw vegetables, hot or cold delicacies, or often they could be chilled leftovers. Quiche de Courgette (page 104), for instance, may be served cold or warm, cut into small segments, or larger slices served for a main course. Ratatouille (page 126) or Tomates à la Provençale (page 109) are also delicious main course meals. Dinner is light and is served late in the evening. It includes fruit, soup and cheese. Desserts are eaten in moderation, although French Patisseries are famous all over the world.

France is also famous for its lovely red and white wines, which are served with any meal.

We sometimes envision French cuisine as a time-consuming and complicated process. Picture instead simplicity and sophistication as you enjoy some of France's favorite dishes.

Photograph Opposite

Top — *Gratin de Légumes (Vegetable Casserole), page 125*
Center — *Quiche de Courgette (Zucchini Quiche), page 104*
Bottom — *Soupe à la Créme Asperges (Cream of Asparagus Soup), page 58*

Insalata Mista

Mixed Salad

1	large head romaine lettuce	1
3	medium-sized ripe tomatoes	3
1	long English cucumber, unpeeled, thinly sliced	1
1	medium onion, thinly sliced into rings	1
1	large lemon, juice of	1
⅓ cup	olive oil	75 mL
2 tbsp.	chopped fresh mint or 1 tsp. (5 mL) dry	30 mL
2 tbsp.	chopped parsley	30 mL
1	garlic clove, minced	1
½ tsp.	salt	2 mL
¼ tsp.	pepper	1 mL

Wash and drain lettuce. Arrange the outside leaves of the lettuce along the rim of a salad bowl. Tear the remainder into bite-sized pieces and place in bowl. Cut tomatoes into wedges and distribute tomatoes and the cucumber over the lettuce. Add separated onion rings.

Combine all remaining ingredients and stir to dissolve the salt.

When ready to serve, drizzle the dressing over the vegetables. Do not toss.

Photograph Opposite

Top — *Tarte Tatin (Apple Pie), page 152*
Center — *Tomates à la Provençale (Stuffed Tomatoes), page 109*
— *Courgette Arlesienne (Zucchini Sauté), page 101*
Bottom — *Salade d' Aubergines et d' Oranges (Eggplant and Orange Salad), page 28*

Insalata Verde

Garden Salad

1	long English cucumber, unpeeled, thinly sliced	1
1	large green bell pepper, cut into thin slices	1
3	medium tomatoes, sliced into thin wedges	3
1	bunch red radishes, thinly sliced	1
½ cup	finely chopped celery	125 mL
⅔ cup	sliced fresh mushrooms	150 mL
2	large carrots, shredded	2
¾ cup	chopped parsley	175 mL
	Lemon Dressing (recipe below)	

Prepare all ingredients and place in a salad bowl.

Toss and chill. Toss with Lemon Dressing when ready to serve.

LEMON DRESSING

½ tsp.	salt	2 mL
½ tsp.	sugar	2 mL
¼ cup	olive oil	60 mL
¼ cup	lemon juice	60 mL

Combine all ingredients. Add to salad.

Michoteta

Vegetable Feta Cheese Salad

Cucumber with feta cheese sauce. Flavorful and tasty! A very attractive salad.

1	**large head romaine lettuce**	1
2	**long English cucumbers, unpeeled, thinly sliced**	2
1	**medium red onion, thinly sliced into rings**	1
½	**green pepper, sliced**	½
1 cup	**crumbled feta cheese**	250 mL
2 tbsp.	**lemon juice**	30 mL
1 tsp.	**chopped fresh oregano or ½ tsp. (2 mL) dried**	5 mL
3 tbsp.	**olive oil**	45 mL
	pepper to taste	
¼ cup	**cold water or as required**	60 mL

Wash and drain romaine and tear into bite-sized pieces. Spread on a large platter. Add the sliced cucumber, then the onion rings and green pepper slices.

Combine in a blender or food processor all remaining ingredients. Blend until smooth. Drizzle the cheese sauce over the vegetables.

See photograph on page 155.

Salata

Greek Salad

This is one version of Greek Salad. Some have romaine lettuce added.

1	**long English cucumber, unpeeled**	1
1	**green bell pepper**	1
2	**large tomatoes, cut into wedges**	2
1	**small onion, thinly sliced**	1
25	**kalamata olives**	25
½ tsp.	**oregano**	2 mL
½ tsp.	**salt**	2 mL
¼ tsp.	**pepper**	1 mL
¼ cup	**lemon juice**	60 mL
¼ cup	**olive oil**	60 mL
¾ cup	**crumbled feta cheese**	175 mL

Slice the cucumber in half lengthwise, then chop into ½" (1.3 cm) cubes. Cut pepper in half, remove seeds and chop into ½" (1.3 cm) cubes. Place in large mixing bowl. Add all remaining ingredients. Toss gently.

See photograph on page 52.

Tomato and Bell Pepper Salad

Morocco

Serves 8

Salad in Morocco consists mostly of crunchy vegetables rather than lettuce. Cumin is a delicious addition to this salad.

3	large tomatoes, cubed	3
2	large green bell peppers, cubed	2
1	English cucumber, unpeeled, thinly sliced	1
2	garlic cloves, minced	2
¼ cup	finely chopped parsley	60 mL
4 tbsp.	olive oil	60 mL
4 tbsp.	lemon juice	60 mL
½ tsp.	salt	2 mL
¾ tsp.	cumin	3 mL
¼ tsp.	pepper	1 mL

Toss all ingredients in a glass salad bowl. Marinate in refrigerator for at least 3 hours.

Insalata Caprese

Italy

Tomato/Mozzarella/Basil Platter

Serves 6

This is a visually delightful salad or appetizer platter.

6	medium-sized ripe tomatoes	6
1 lb.	mozzarella cheese, sliced	454 g
2	medium purple onions, sliced into rings	2
¼ cup	olive oil	60 mL
¼ tsp.	salt	1 mL
¼ tsp.	pepper	1 mL
1 tsp.	oregano	5 mL
	fresh basil leaves for garnish	

Wash tomatoes well, dry and polish. Cut lengthwise, leaving every two slices joined together at the base.

Insert a slice of cheese and some onion rings between each two-slice section.

Arrange on a platter, stacking side by side at an angle.

Drizzle oil over all, sprinkle with salt, pepper and oregano. Garnish with basil leaves along the edges of the platter.

See photograph on front cover.

Tabouli

This is Dana's favorite salad. It is the queen of Lebanese salads, you may never want a plain salad again! This salad is also popular in other Middle Eastern countries.

3	large bunches of parsley	3
⅓ cup	bulgar (crushed wheat)	75 mL
2 cups	water	500 mL
4	green onions, with ends	4
¼ cup	chopped fresh mint or 2 tbsp. (30 mL) dry	60 mL
2	large tomatoes, finely diced	2
1½ tsp.	salt	7 mL
¼ tsp.	pepper	1 mL
⅓ cup	lemon juice or to taste	75 mL
¼ cup	olive oil or vegetable oil	60 mL
	romaine lettuce leaves for serving	

Wash parsley well, drain and shake out excess moisture.

In a large mixing bowl, soak crushed wheat in water for 2 minutes. Drain well and set aside while preparing other ingredients.

Remove stems from parsley and discard. Chop parsley very finely (3 bunches should equal 5 cups (1.25 L)). Add to wheat.

Finely chop onions and add to the wheat mixture along with the remaining ingredients, except for lettuce.

If not serving immediately, do not add tomatoes and onions; add just before serving. Toss well.

Serve with romaine lettuce leaves. Tear leaves into bite-sized pieces and use to scoop up salad for eating.

VARIATION:
You may want to add finely chopped romaine lettuce and cucumber.

Saffi

Serves 4-6

Amy loved the traditional Tabouli until she was introduced to this salad, which is also sometimes called Tabouli. Seen quite often in deli showcases in supermarkets and health food stores, it is very tasty and nutritious. This salad has more bulgar and less parsley than the classic Lebanese Tabouli.

1 cup	cooked chickpeas	250 mL
1½ cups	bulgar (crushed wheat)	375 mL
1 cup	cold water	250 mL
½ cup	finely chopped green onions	125 mL
1	long English cucumber, finely chopped	1
2 tbsp.	chopped fresh mint or 1 tbsp. (15 mL) dry	30 mL
1 cup	finely chopped parsley	250 mL
⅓ cup	lemon juice	75 mL
⅓ cup	olive oil	75 mL
1 tsp.	salt	5 mL
¼ tsp.	pepper	1 mL
¼ tsp.	cinnamon	1 mL
	romaine lettuce, cabbage or grape vine leaves for serving	

Drain chickpeas.

Place the bulgar and cold water in a large salad bowl. Stir and set aside for 15-20 minutes. Add chickpeas and all remaining ingredients, except for lettuce, toss well.

Serve with romaine lettuce leaves, parboiled cabbage, or fresh tender grape vine leaves. Tear leaves into bite-sized pieces and use to scoop up salad for eating.

VARIATION:

Any or all of these vegetables may be added — finely chopped celery, green or red peppers and tomatoes.

See photograph on page 88.

Bulgar with Vegetable Salad

Greece

Serves 6-8

This salad can serve as a hot meal or a cold salad.

2 cups	water or vegetable stock (page 72)	500 mL
¾ tsp.	salt	3 mL
1 cup	bulgar (crushed wheat)	250 mL
	Mustard Dressing (recipe below)	
1 cup	canned marinated artichoke hearts, reserve liquid	250 mL
1	large carrot, shredded	1
2	large celery stalks, thinly sliced	2
1	green pepper, seeded and diced	1
3	green onions including tops, thinly sliced	3
½ cup	chopped parsley	125 mL
8	lettuce leaves	8
3	eggs, hard-boiled and quartered	3
2	medium tomatoes, cut into wedges	2
4 oz.	sharp Cheddar cheese, cut into julienne strips	115 g
10	black or green olives	10

Combine water and salt in a 3-quart (3 L) saucepan, bring to boil. Stir in bulgar. Reduce heat, cover and simmer for 10 minutes.

Prepare Mustard Dressing. Add drained marinade from artichokes to the dressing, mixing well. Dice artichokes and set aside.

Turn cooked bulgar into a large bowl, add dressing, stir gently.

If serving hot, stir in artichokes, carrots, celery, green pepper, onions and parsley. Arrange lettuce on a serving platter and mound the bulgar mixture on top. Surround with eggs. Sprinkle with cheese and garnish with the olives.

For a cold salad. After adding the dressing, stir in the vegetables. Cover and refrigerate for 2 hours before serving or until the following day. Mound bulgar salad on lettuce leaves and garnish as above.

MUSTARD DRESSING

4 tbsp.	lemon juice	60 mL
4 tbsp.	olive oil	60 mL
1 tsp.	basil	5 mL
1 tsp.	oregano	5 mL
½ tsp.	pepper	2 mL
2	garlic cloves, minced	2
1 tbsp.	Dijon mustard	15 mL

Combine all ingredients in a bowl and mix well.

See photograph on page 51.

Andalusian Salad

Rice Salad

This salad has Spanish influences but it was adopted by the French. It comes from the south of France.

⅓ cup	thinly sliced radishes	75 mL
1 cup	finely chopped celery	250 mL
¼ cup	finely chopped parsley	60 mL
⅓ cup	chopped green onions	75 mL
2 cups	cooked brown rice, cold	500 mL
½ cup	raisins	125 mL
½ cup	sunflower seeds or pumpkin seeds	125 mL
½ tsp.	salt	2 mL
¼ tsp.	pepper	1 mL
½ tsp.	sugar	2 mL
2 tbsp.	red wine vinegar	30 mL
¼ cup	olive oil	60 mL
1 cup	finely sliced mushrooms	250 mL
1	head butter lettuce	1

In a large salad bowl, combine first 7 ingredients, set aside.

In small bowl, combine the salt, pepper, sugar and vinegar. Mix well. Add oil and stir. Drizzle dressing over the vegetables.

Just before serving, add the mushrooms and toss gently. Arrange in lettuce leaves or serve from a salad bowl.

Salatat Batata

Potato Salad with Lemon   Serves 4

This is another of Dana's favorite salads.

6	medium potatoes	6
½ cup	finely chopped parsley	125 mL
½ cup	finely chopped green onions	125 mL
2	garlic cloves, minced	2
½ tsp.	salt	2 mL
¼ tsp.	pepper	1 mL
¼ cup	lemon juice	60 mL
¼ cup	olive oil	60 mL

Boil potatoes with skins on. Let cool. Peel and cut into ½" (1.3 cm) cubes. Place in salad bowl. Add parsley and onions. Add all remaining ingredients, toss well. Cover and refrigerate. Serve cold.

VARIATIONS:
1. Toss in 2-3 hard-boiled eggs, coarsely chopped.
2. A chopped green or red pepper adds a welcome flavor when tossed into this salad.

Pasta and Green Bean Salad

Serves 4-6

Any variety of pasta can be used in this tasty salad.

10 oz.	penne or other pasta	285 g
½ lb.	green beans, cut into 2" (5 cm) lengths	250 g
¼ cup	olive oil	60 mL
½ cup	red wine vinegar	125 mL
1 tsp.	Dijon mustard	5 mL
½ tsp.	salt	2 mL
¼ tsp.	pepper	1 mL
1 cup	pitted black olives	250 mL
5	green onions, cut lengthwise then chopped into 2" (5 cm) lengths	5
¼ cup	grated Parmesan cheese	60 mL

Cook pasta following package directions. During the last 7-8 minutes of cooking time, add the beans. Drain well. Rinse with cold water. Drain again.

Combine oil, vinegar, mustard, salt and pepper in a large salad bowl. Mix well.

Add pasta, beans, olives and green onions. Toss gently. Sprinkle with Parmesan cheese.

VARIATIONS:
1. Replace vinegar with lemon juice.
2. ½ tsp. (2 mL) of rosemary may be added with the seasonings.
3. Red or green peppers can replace the beans however DO NOT cook them with the pasta; toss them in the marinade with the cold pasta.

Salatat Lubi mah Thoum

Green Bean and Garlic Salad

This salad is so wonderful and tangy.

2	red peppers	2
1 lb.	green beans, cut in half	500 g
	water	
8 tbsp.	olive oil	125 mL
10	large garlic cloves	10
2 tbsp.	vinegar	30 mL
2½ tbsp.	lemon juice	37 mL
6 cups	endive, torn into bite-sized pieces	1.5 L
2 tbsp.	chopped basil	30 mL
¼ cup	pine nuts, toasted	60 mL
	salt and pepper to taste	

Heat oven to 350°F (180°C).

Cook peppers on cookie sheet under broiler until blackened on all sides. Place in paper bag to steam for 10 minutes. Peel, seed and slice thinly. Set aside.

Cook green beans in large pot of water until just tender. Drain. Pour cold water over beans to refresh. Drain well.

Heat 2 tbsp. (30 mL) of the olive oil in a small heavy ovenproof skillet over medium heat. Add garlic cloves and sauté until golden brown, stirring occasionally. Cover and place in oven. Cook until cloves are tender, about 10 minutes. Cool and chop.

Whisk remaining 6 tbsp. (95 mL) of olive oil, vinegar and lemon juice in a small bowl to make a dressing. Place the endive in a large bowl. Add some of the dressing to taste. Divide the endive among 6-8 plates. Add to the remaining dressing, the peppers, green beans, garlic, basil and toasted pine nuts and toss. Season with salt and pepper. Use this mixture to top the endive.

VARIATIONS:
1. In place of endive, any variety of lettuce can be used.
2. In place of green beans, use any dry bean or pea that has been cooked.

Salatat Fasoolia

Beans in Lemon Sauce

1 cup	dried white beans, soaked overnight	250 mL
5 cups	water	1.25 L
1	red pepper, diced	1
½ cup	julienned onion	125 mL
¼ cup	lemon juice	60 mL
½ tsp.	salt	2 mL
¼ cup	olive oil	60 mL
2 tbsp.	chopped parsley	30 mL

Drain beans and place in large saucepan. Add the water and bring to a boil, lower heat, cover and cook slowly for approximately 1 hour, or until tender. Drain well.

Place beans in a salad bowl, add all remaining ingredients.

Toss, serve chilled.

VARIATIONS:
1. Other vegetables such as sliced cucumber, radishes or cooked cubed potatoes can be added.
2. Minced garlic cloves and ½ tsp. (2 mL) oregano may be tossed with the salad.

Salatat Fasoolia

Three Bean Salad

In North America, marinated bean salads have become staples at picnics and family gatherings. You will want to add this Lebanese version to your recipe collection.

2 cups	cooked kidney beans	500 mL
2 cups	cooked chickpeas	500 mL
1 cup	cooked lima beans	250 mL
¼ cup	finely chopped parsley	60 mL
1	small red onion, sliced into rings	1
4	garlic cloves, minced	4
⅓ cup	lemon juice	75 mL
⅓ cup	olive oil	75 mL
1 tsp.	salt	5 mL
½ tsp.	pepper	2 mL

Rinse all beans in cold water. Drain and place in a salad bowl. Add parsley and onion rings. Add all remaining ingredients. Toss gently.

Salad can be served immediately or can be placed in the refrigerator to marinate for 4-5 hours for added flavor.

Soups

Greece

Olives are Greece's oldest cultivated food product, dating back 4,000 years. In ancient Greece, olive oil was the primary fat. During that time, the Greeks considered it a sacred commodity, a symbol of peace, fertility, strength and purity. They traded their liquid gold for foods they could not grow in their own rocky soil. It was the Greeks who introduced olive oil to Italy, France, Spain and northern Africa.

Olive oil is an essential ingredient in Greek cooking and is a staple in every home. Another staple is feta cheese. It is used as a table cheese, eaten with fruit, in salads and as part of many main courses. This cheese is rapidly gaining popularity in the Western world.

Other important ingredients in this cuisine include herbs, spices, lemon juice and olives. Basil and oregano are favorite herbs, cinnamon and coriander are also used liberally.

Greece is self sufficient in wheat, rice and potatoes. Many foods are grown primarily for export, such as grains, currants, grapes, olives, nuts, citrus fruits and figs. Lentils, one of the favorite foods of the ancient Greek civilization, were known as everyday food for the lower classes. Chickpeas were also considered to be common food and only the poor made use of them. They were thought to promote strength and their Latin name, *Cicer*, derives from the Greek *kiker*, meaning strength.

Soups of all kinds are an important part of the Greek diet. One of the most popular, Avgolemono Soup (page 55) is made with lemon and served hot or cold. Breakfast is served early and may consist of cheese, fruit and eggs. A heavier lunch is served in the late afternoon; the evening meal is light.

Vegetables are plentiful. Eggplant and artichokes are most often associated with Greek food. A wonderful example is Moussaka (page 132). A traditional accompaniment to many meals is rice pilaf and the Greek pasta, orzo. This pasta resembles rice and is often cooked with soups, salads or main courses.

Ouzo, a liqueur, colorless and licorice-anise-flavored, is the drink of the land here. It is generally served with water, then the color is milky; only the brave will have it on the rocks or straight.

Photograph Opposite

Top   — *Vegetable Kebabs, page 96*
Center — *Bulgar with Vegetable Salad, page 42*
Bottom — *Koukia Yiahnt (Fava Bean Stew), page 123*

Shourabit Laban

Yogurt Soup

Serves 8

Fresh mint is a must for this recipe. Serve on a cool day.

4 cups	yogurt	1 L
4 cups	water	1 L
½ cup	rice	125 mL
1	egg	1
1 tsp.	salt	5 mL
	fresh mint for garnish	

Place yogurt in a heavy saucepan, beat with fork or beater until smooth. Add water, stir well, set aside.

Rinse and drain rice, place in a small bowl, add egg and mix well. Add this mixture to the yogurt along with the salt.

Place saucepan over medium heat. Stir soup constantly with a wooden spoon, being careful not to let it scorch. Bring to a boil. Turn heat down slightly and cook for 15-20 minutes until rice is tender. Stir occasionally.

Serve hot or cold with a pinch of fresh chopped mint sprinkled over each serving.

VARIATIONS:
1. Break eggs and drop them into the soup when soup is almost cooked. Do not stir as yolk will break.
2. Drop any chopped vegetables into the soup just before soup is cooked.
3. Prepare Bulgar Balls (page 54) and cook in the boiling soup.

Photograph Opposite

Top — Soupa de Almendras (Almond Soup), page 57
Center — Tzakziki (Yogurt Cucumber Dip), page 24
Bottom — Salata (Greek Salad), page 38

Zonkol bi Laban

Bulgar Balls in Cold Yogurt

Serves 6

A cool soup on a warm summer day.

1	recipe of Bulgar Balls (see below)	1
5 cups	water	1.25 L
	dash of salt	
2	garlic cloves, crushed	2
1 tsp.	salt	5 mL
4-5 cups	cold yogurt	1-1.25 L
2 tbsp.	fresh mint or 1 tbsp. (15 mL) dry	30 mL

Shape bulgar dough into small marble-sized balls. Set aside. Place water in saucepan and add a dash of salt. Bring to a boil. Add the bulgar balls and cook for 10-15 minutes at a steady low boil. Drain and set aside to cool.

Combine the garlic, salt and yogurt in a serving bowl. Blend thoroughly with a fork. Add bulgar balls and mix gently. Sprinkle mint over top.

See photograph on page 88.

Kibbi Tahili

Lebanon

Bulgar Balls

Serves 6-8

1½ cups	bulgar (crushed wheat)	375 mL
2 cups	warm water	500 mL
1 tsp.	salt	5 mL
¼ tsp.	pepper	1 mL
⅓ cup	flour	75 mL

Soak bulgar in water for 2 minutes. Add salt, pepper and flour. Knead well. If too thick, add a little more warm water to the mixture so the dough is pliable. It should be the consistency of pie dough.

With dampened hands make marble-sized balls from the mixture. Place them on a cookie sheet until all the dough has been rolled.

VARIATIONS:
1. Use for Bulgar Balls in Cold Yogurt, (above).
2. Use for Yogurt Soup, (page 53).
3. Bulgar balls may be cooked in any soup or stew for 10 minutes, stirring occasionally.

Soupa Avgolemono Kria

Greece

Cold Avgolemono Soup

Serves 6

A delicious lemon-flavored Greek soup traditionally made with chicken broth, this recipe is made with vegetable stock. Serve hot or cold.

4½ cups	vegetable stock (page 72) or water	1.125 L
½ cup	rice, rinsed and drained	125 mL
½ tsp.	salt	2 mL
4	eggs	4
2	lemons, juice of	2
2 cups	heavy cream (for cold soup only)	500 mL

Place the vegetable stock in a 3-quart (3 L) saucepan. Add the rice and salt. Bring to a boil, lower heat to medium and cook for 25 minutes. Set aside.

In a large bowl, beat the eggs well, gradually adding lemon juice while beating. Slowly add the hot broth and rice to the egg sauce, beating vigorously. Return mixture to saucepan, heat and stir until thickened. **Do not allow to boil.** Remove from heat. The soup may be served hot at this time.

For cold soup, cool the soup. Just before serving, beat the cream until thick; fold into the soup and serve.

VARIATION:

1. Top each serving with a tablespoon (15 mL) of whipped cream instead of folding all of the cream into the soup.

Watercress Vichyssoise

Chilled Watercress Soup

This lovely classic French soup is an elegant variation of the simple and delicious potato and leek soup.

6 cups	vegetable stock (page 72) or water	1.5 L
2	medium potatoes, diced	2
3 cups	coarsely chopped leeks	750 mL
2 cups	lightly packed watercress sprigs	500 mL
½ cup	whipping cream	125 mL
1¼ tsp.	salt	6 mL
½ tsp.	white pepper	2 mL
	watercress sprigs for garnish	

Bring stock to a boil in a large saucepan. Add potatoes and leeks. Bring to a boil, then reduce heat. Cover and simmer for 20 minutes.

Add watercress. Let simmer for 3 minutes. Remove from heat. While still warm, place soup in processor or blender and blend in batches. Place in a serving bowl. Stir in the cream, salt and pepper. Chill.

Garnish each serving with sprigs of watercress.

VARIATIONS:
1. To serve hot, remove soup from heat just before stirring in cream. Stir in cream all at once or ladle soup into bowls and drizzle cream into soup with a large spoon, this creates a swirling pattern on the soup.
2. If watercress is not available, make this soup without it and serve hot potato and leek soup or chilled vichyssoise.

Soupa de Almendras

Almond Soup

Serves 6-8

2 tbsp.	butter	30 mL
1 tbsp.	grated onion	15 mL
2 tbsp.	flour	30 mL
6 cups	vegetable stock (page 72) or water	1.5 L
1½ cups	blanched almonds	375 mL
⅛ tsp.	nutmeg	0.5 mL
1 tsp.	salt	5 mL
½ tsp.	pepper	2 mL
⅔ cup	heavy cream	150 mL
2	egg yolks, slightly beaten	2
1 tsp.	grated lemon rind	5 mL
	watercress leaves	
	nutmeg for garnish	

Melt butter in a large saucepan, add onions and cook on medium heat until onion is wilted; blend in flour. Stir in vegetable stock. Cook, stirring, until smooth and boiling.

In a processor or nut chopper, finely chop almonds to resemble a paste. Add to soup along with seasonings, stirring with a fork to break up the almond paste. Cover and simmer for 15 minutes.

Combine cream, egg yolks and lemon rind. Pour slowly into hot mixture, stirring constantly. Heat but do not bring to a boil.

Serve garnished with sprigs of watercress and a sprinkle of nutmeg.

See photograph on page 52.

Soupe à la Crème Asperges

Cream of Asparagus Soup

A delightful and delectable soup.

3 tbsp.	unsalted butter	45 mL
1 cup	minced onion	250 mL
4 cups	vegetable stock (page 72) or water	1 L
1¼ lbs.	thin asparagus, trimmed, fresh or frozen	625 g
¼ cup	whipping cream	60 mL
¾ tsp.	salt	3 mL
¼ tsp.	white pepper	1 mL
	fresh lemon (optional)	

Melt butter in a 3-quart (3 L) saucepan on medium heat, add the onions and cook on high heat until lightly browned. Add the vegetable stock, bring to a boil.

Cut the tips of the asparagus approximately 3" (7 cm) in length. Set aside.

Chop remainder of asparagus in processor, blending with a little of the broth to aid the process. Add this to the boiling broth. Cover and boil gently for about 30 minutes.

Add asparagus tips, simmer for approximately 10 minutes, until tips are just tender.

Stir in the cream, add seasonings.

Serve warm or cold with a squeeze of lemon juice for each serving.

See photograph on page 33.

Zuppa di Fagioli con la Pasta

Bean Soup with Pasta

Italy

Serves 5

A wonderful meal in itself or with crusty Italian bread.

6 cups	vegetable stock (page 72) or water	1.5 L
1¼ cups	dried navy beans, soaked overnight	300 mL
1	large onion, chopped	1
2	large tomatoes, chopped or 1 cup (250 mL) tomato sauce	2
2	celery stalks, chopped	2
2	garlic cloves, chopped	2
1 tsp.	salt	5 mL
¼ tsp.	pepper	1 mL
½ cup	uncooked macaroni (elbows, small bows or shells)	125 mL
	grated Parmesan cheese	

Place stock in a large soup pot. Add drained beans and bring to a boil. Cover and cook on low heat for 30 minutes.

Add the onion, tomatoes, celery, garlic, salt and pepper. Heat to boiling; reduce heat. Cover and simmer until beans are tender, approximately 2 hours.

Stir macaroni into soup. Cover and simmer until macaroni is tender, 10-15 minutes. Sprinkle with the cheese.

Minestrone

Vegetable Soup

An Italian classic. Very hearty and thick. Delicious served as lunch with Focaccia (page 93), a flat Italian bread.

1 cup	dried beans, (kidney, navy, chickpeas or a mixture), soaked overnight	250 mL
6 cups	water	1.5 L
1 cup	fresh string beans, cut into 1½" (4 cm) lengths	250 mL
4	garlic cloves, minced	4
1 cup	shredded spinach or cabbage	250 mL
1 cup	diced tomatoes	250 mL
1 cup	diced carrots	250 mL
1 cup	diced onions	250 mL
1 cup	chopped celery	250 mL
¼ cup	olive oil	60 mL
1 tbsp.	chopped Italian parsley	15 mL
½ tsp.	pesto (page 139)	2 mL
1½ cups	tomato sauce	375 mL
¾ cup	whole-wheat macaroni salt and pepper to taste	175 mL

Drain beans, place in a large saucepan with the water. Bring to a boil, cover and cook for 45 minutes, or until tender.

Place all vegetables and the oil into a large soup pot. Sauté for 5 minutes, stirring constantly.

Place half of the cooked beans and some liquid in a blender or food processor, blend until smooth. Add bean purée, vegetables, parsley, pesto and tomato sauce to the cooked beans and liquid. Simmer for 45-60 minutes, then add macaroni and salt and pepper to taste. Simmer for 15 minutes, or until macaroni is tender.

Add more water to thin the soup if necessary.

Potaje Murciano

Kidney Bean Soup

A thick and hearty soup from Valencia, this makes a good meal.

1 cup	dried red kidney beans, soaked overnight	250 mL
1	bay leaf	1
½ tsp.	salt	2 mL
5 cups	vegetable stock (page 72) or water	1.25 L
1 cup	rice	250 mL
½ lb.	green beans, cut into 2" (5 cm) lengths	250 g
3 tbsp.	olive oil	45 mL
1	medium onion, cut in half and sliced	1
3	garlic cloves, minced	3
4	tomatoes, skinned and chopped	4
¼ tsp.	cumin	1 mL
1½ tsp.	brown sugar	7 mL
1 tbsp.	wine vinegar	15 mL
	freshly ground black pepper	

Drain kidney beans and place in a large saucepan. Add the bay leaf, salt and the stock. Bring to a boil. Cover and cook on medium-low heat for 1-1½ hours until beans are just tender.

Add rice, green beans and more stock if required. Simmer for 15 minutes.

Heat oil in a skillet and sauté the onions and garlic. When the onions are softened, add remaining ingredients and season to taste. Stir well and cook gently for 5 minutes. Add this mixture to the beans and rice. Cook for a further 5 minutes. The soup should be quite thick.

Serve with bread.

Shourabit addas mah Ruz

Lentil Rice Soup

Lebanon

Serves 8-10

This soup is the soup of the day, every day, at the Cedars Restaurant.

1 cup	lentils	250 mL
6 cups	vegetable stock (page 72) or water	1.5 L
½ cup	rice	125 mL
1	large onion, chopped	1
2	medium carrots, diced	2
2	celery stalks, diced	2
	salt and pepper to taste	
1	lemon, cut in half	1

Rinse and drain lentils, place in a soup pot with the water, bring to a boil, cover and simmer for approximately 1 hour until lentils are tender, almost mushy. Stir occasionally.

Rinse and drain rice, add to lentils, stir, bring to a boil. Cover and simmer, stirring occasionally, for 25 minutes. Add remaining ingredients except lemon. Cook on medium heat for 10 minutes more, stirring occasionally. Carrots should still be a little bit firm. Add more stock to thin the soup if necessary.

Serve with a squeeze of lemon juice on top of each serving.

Shourabit Hommous

Chickpea Soup

Lebanon

Serves 4-6

4 cups	chickpeas, cooked	1 L
2 cups	vegetable stock (page 72) or water	500 mL
1 cup	grated carrots	250 mL
½ cup	finely chopped celery	125 mL
¼ cup	chopped parsley	60 mL
1 tsp.	oregano	5 mL
1 tsp.	salt	5 mL
½ tsp.	pepper	2 mL
4 tbsp.	fresh yogurt	60 mL

Blend all ingredients, except yogurt, in a blender or food processor until smooth.

Place in large saucepan, bring to a boil on medium heat. Lower heat, cover and simmer for 10 minutes, stirring occasionally. Remove from heat.

Garnish each serving with a tablespoon (15 mL) of yogurt.

Vegetarian El Harirah Soup

Morocco

Serves 8-10

This soup is famous in Morocco. It keeps well in the refrigerator for several days.

1 cup	barley	250 mL
½ cup	lentils	125 mL
1 cup	chickpeas	250 mL
3 tbsp.	vegetable oil	45 mL
3 cups	chopped onions	750 mL
1 cup	chopped celery	250 mL
1 cup	chopped carrots	250 mL
1 tbsp.	turmeric	15 mL
8 cups	vegetable stock (page 72) or water	2 L
	salt and pepper to taste	
½ cup	rice	125 mL
1½ tbsp.	flour	22 mL
1	egg, beaten slightly	1
	lemon juice or vinegar to taste	
¼ cup	chopped fresh coriander	60 mL

Soak barley, lentils and chickpeas overnight in plenty of water.

Heat oil in a large soup pot over medium heat. Add onions, celery and carrots. Cook and stir until onions are transparent. Sprinkle with turmeric. Stir in the stock, add salt and pepper. Bring to a boil. Partly cover and simmer, skimming off the foam. Cook for 30 minutes.

Drain the barley, lentils and chickpeas. Rinse and drain the rice and add all of this to the soup. Cook for 45 minutes.

Place flour in a small mixing bowl and blend with a little of the soup. Add to the soup in the pot; stir. Beat the egg with a little of the soup liquid and add to the pot. Bring soup just to the boiling point but do not boil. Add lemon and coriander and serve.

If soup is not served immediately it will thicken. It will then be necessary to add a little more vegetable stock or water to thin it down.

Zuppa di Verdura

Vegetable Soup

Serves 8-10

The variety of ingredients in this soup results in a subtle blend of flavors.

¼ cup	olive oil	60 mL
3	large carrots, diced	3
3	medium potatoes, diced	3
1	small cauliflower, divided into florets	1
2	leeks, chopped	2
2	celery stalks, chopped	2
1	medium onion, sliced	1
5	romaine lettuce leaves, shredded	5
½ cup	green peas	125 mL
1 cup	green beans, chopped	250 mL
	salt and pepper to taste	
8 cups	vegetable stock (page 72)	2 L
	toasted bread	
	grated Parmesan cheese	

Combine oil and vegetables in a large soup pot, and sauté on medium heat until they soften and begin to change color. Season with salt and pepper. Add only 2 cups (500 mL) of stock, cover and simmer on very low heat for approximately 25 minutes. Add the remaining stock, bring to a boil, cover and simmer for a further 25 minutes.

Serve very hot with slices of toasted bread in each bowl and sprinkle with plenty of Parmesan cheese.

This soup can be refrigerated, covered, for 2-3 days.

Escudella de Catalonia

Spain

Catalonian Vegetable Soup

Serves 4-6

A tasty, thick soup with vegetables and saffron.

4¼ cups	vegetable stock (page 72)	1.06 L
3	garlic cloves, chopped	3
1	large onion, chopped	1
2 cups	finely diced turnip	500 mL
2	celery stalks, finely diced	2
2	medium potatoes, finely diced	2
2	carrots, finely diced	2
⅓ cup	long-grain rice	75 mL
½ tsp.	powdered saffron	2 mL
	salt to taste	
½ tsp.	pepper	2 mL

Place the stock in a large saucepan over high heat. Add garlic and all the vegetables. Bring to a boil. Cover and simmer for 15 minutes. Add rice and saffron and cook for a further 25-30 minutes until rice is tender. If soup becomes too thick add a little boiling vegetable stock. Season to taste. Serve hot with lots of crusty bread.

Shourabit Milookhiyya

Egyptian Milookhiyya Soup

Milookhiyya is a leafy vegetable available fresh or dried in Middle Eastern stores. It is sometimes called Spanish okra. Fresh sorrel or spinach can be substituted, but should not be soaked.

2	large onions, quartered	2
3	garlic cloves, minced	3
2	celery stalks with leaves, chopped	2
¼ cup	coarsely chopped parsley	60 mL
4	large ripe tomatoes, chopped	4
1 tbsp.	salt	15 mL
6	peppercorns, lightly crushed or ½ tsp. (2 mL) pepper	6
6	whole allspice, lightly crushed or ½ tsp. (2 mL) ground allspice	6
8 cups	vegetable stock (page 72) or water	2 L
1½ cups	dried milookhiyya, crumbled	375 mL
	warm water to cover	
1 tbsp.	lemon juice	15 mL
3 tbsp.	butter	45 mL
4	garlic cloves, minced	4
1 tsp.	dry coriander	5 mL
¼ tsp.	allspice	1 mL
⅛ tsp.	cayenne pepper or to taste	0.5 mL

Combine first 9 ingredients in a large soup pot. Bring to a boil on high heat. Cover and lower heat to a gentle boil and cook for 25 minutes.

While soup is cooking, combine milookhiyya, water and lemon juice. Let soak for 20 minutes, or until doubled in bulk. Drain and add to the soup. Bring to a boil and cook over medium heat for 25 minutes, uncovered.

In a small frying pan, melt butter; add remaining ingredients. Sauté until garlic is just golden brown. Add to soup. Cook for 2-3 minutes.

Serve on a cold winter day with crisp pita bread dried in the oven.

Shourabit Thoum

Spicy Garlic Soup

Garlic has a long history in Egyptian cooking. Slaves building the pyramids were fed garlic to give them physical strength. It has also been credited for centuries with medicinal powers ranging from cures for colds, consumption and open cuts to toothaches. Here it is simply and distinctively featured in this flavorful soup.

¼ cup	**butter**	**60 mL**
½ cup	**finely chopped garlic**	**125 mL**
3 tbsp.	**flour**	**45 mL**
3 cups	**vegetable stock (page 72)**	**750 mL**
	cayenne pepper to taste	
	salt to taste	
1 tsp.	**chopped fresh coriander**	**5 mL**

Melt butter in heavy 1½-quart (1.5 L) saucepan over medium heat. Add garlic and sauté for 3-4 minutes until golden brown. Add flour and stir constantly until mixture is lightly browned. Add the stock and bring to a boil, stirring constantly. Reduce heat and simmer for 15 minutes, stirring occasionally. Season with cayenne pepper and salt.

Garnish with coriander just before serving.

Leftovers can be refrigerated then reheated before serving

Italy

To most North Americans, the thought of pasta conjures up an image of spaghetti or lasagne bathed in tomato sauce. Italians, however, envision more glorious preparations. Pasta is economical, nutritious, convenient, and easily adaptable to everyday gourmet tastes. It can be topped with sauces, added to soups or tossed in salads. Fresh pasta comes in a variety of shapes, colors and flavors. Supermarkets have dry pasta in tantalizing forms such as rigatoni, perciatelli, tripoline and rolelle.

Northern Italy is the richest part of the country, with the best agricultural land, where wheat and rice are grown. Italians are frugal and hardworking people, trying to get as much as they can from the soil. Italy produces fruit, wine, olive oil and cheese. It is also famous for its tomatoes, peppers, pasta dishes, spices, herbs, garlic and a variety of beans.

Vegetables are an essential part of the diet. This is one country in which it would be easy to eat well without eating meat. Italians have always made abundant and imaginative use of pasta, rice, beans, cheese, bread, eggs and vegetables. What Italians do with vegetables is truly amazing. They serve them raw with dips, turn them into soups and salads, mix them with rice or pasta, use them to top a pizza, transform them into gourmet meals or side dishes. No wonder that their diet is one of the healthiest in the world. They boast a low rate of heart disease and cancer.

Breakfast is served early, lunch may be a salad with a large array of courses served in the late afternoon. Dinner is light and is served late in the evening with fruits, cheese or salad.

Italians know how to accentuate the natural goodness of fresh ingredients in many innovative ways. This is apparent in the preparation of their sauces and the way they creatively combine herbs and spices. Basil is a very popular herb and so is flat-leafed parsley which is tasty and aromatic. Nutmeg, oregano, rosemary, marjoram and sage are always within easy reach in the kitchen and play a very important roll in Italian cuisine. Italians pride themselves on the wines they produce and rightfully so. Italy produces some of the best wines in the world. Vegetarian lasagne or Pizza (page 136) go well with a glass of red or white wine.

Photograph Opposite

Top — *Funghi Peperoni (Mushroom and Pepper Sauté), page 82*
Center — *Focaccia (Italian Flat Bread), page 93*
Bottom — *Spaghetti con le Melanzane (Spaghetti with Eggplant), page 141*

Soupe à l'Oignon

France

French Onion Soup

Serves 6-8

The French are renowned for their onion soup. This is one version of many.

2	large onions, cut in half and thinly sliced	2
2	garlic cloves, minced	2
4 tbsp.	butter	60 mL
	salt and pepper to taste	
1 tbsp.	flour	15 mL
6 cups	vegetable stock (page 72) or water	1.5 L
½	bay leaf	½
¼ tsp.	dried thyme	1 mL
8	slices French bread, cut into 1" (2.5 cm) slices	8
½ cup	grated Gruyère or Swiss cheese	125 mL

Place onions, garlic and butter in a large saucepan. Add salt and pepper to taste. Cook over medium heat, stirring, for about 15 minutes, until onions are golden brown.

Sprinkle onion mixture with the flour and cook, stirring, for 3 minutes. Add the stock, bay leaf and thyme. Cover and simmer for 30-40 minutes.

Preheat oven to 350°F (180°C).

Arrange bread on a baking sheet and bake until lightly browned. Turn bread over and toast the other side.

Pour the hot soup into a 1½-quart (1.5 L) casserole or into individual onion soup bowls. Float the toast on top of the soup and sprinkle with cheese.

Place the casserole or bowls in the oven on a baking sheet to catch the drippings. Broil until cheese melts and is golden brown.

Photograph Opposite

Top — Fettuccine al Pesto (Fettuccine with Pesto), page 138
Bottom — Bruschetta con Pomodoro (Bruschetta with Tomatoes), page 20

Vegetable Stock

Lebanon

Makes about 4 quarts (4 L)

This stock makes every dish you prepare very tasty and nutritious.

¼ cup	butter or vegetable oil	60 mL
4	medium carrots, chopped	4
2	medium onions, chopped	2
3	large celery stalks with leaves, chopped	3
1	medium turnip, diced	1
2	garlic cloves, crushed (optional)	2
12 cups	water	3 L
2 tsp.	salt or to taste	10 mL
1	bay leaf	1
4	large parsley sprigs	4
½ tsp.	thyme	2 mL
½ tsp.	pepper	2 mL

Melt butter in a large soup pot over medium heat. Add all chopped vegetables. Cook for 10 minutes stirring occasionally.

Add water and all remaining ingredients. Bring to a boil. Reduce heat, cover and simmer for ½ hour. Strain through a sieve, pushing some of the vegetables through the fine holes with the back of a large spoon.

Stir. Cool and store in refrigerator or freeze for future use.

For flavorful and nutritious meals, add stock in place of water to all soups, stews and casserole dishes.

VARIATION:
Vegetables of your choice may be substituted or added to this recipe.

Side Dishes

Esparragos Con Guisantes

Asparagus with Peas

Serves 4

In southern Spain, asparagus is plentiful and in some places grows wild.

2½ cups	water	625 mL
½ tsp.	salt	2 mL
1 lb.	fresh tender asparagus tips	454 g
3 cups	green peas, fresh or frozen	750 mL

HERBED WHITE SAUCE

½ cup	butter	125 mL
2 tbsp.	flour	30 mL
1¼ cup	milk	300 mL
¼ tsp.	salt	1 mL
¼ tsp.	pepper	1 mL
1 tbsp.	chopped mint	15 mL
1 tbsp.	chopped parsley	15 mL

In a large saucepan, boil the water and add salt.

Add asparagus and cook for 2-3 minutes. Drain thoroughly, add the peas. Set aside.

To make sauce, melt butter in small saucepan on medium heat. Add the flour stirring constantly for 1-2 minutes. Gradually add milk while stirring, cooking until a smooth sauce is obtained. Add salt, pepper and herbs.

Add sauce to the asparagus and peas, return to heat, cook gently for approximately 15 minutes, or until vegetables are tender, stirring frequently. Add a little water if sauce becomes too thick.

Serve as an appetizer with bread or as a side dish.

Artichauts à l'Orange

France

Artichokes with Oranges

Serves 6

This combination makes a lovely side dish.

2	**lemons, juice of**	2
15	**small artichoke hearts, frozen**	15
1½ cups	**water**	375 mL
¼ cup	**vegetable oil**	60 mL
¼ tsp.	**saffron**	1 mL
1 tsp.	**salt**	5 mL
¼ tsp.	**pepper**	1 mL
3	**oranges, cut into ½" (1.3 cm) slices, seeds removed**	3

Place lemon juice and the thawed artichokes in a mixing bowl.

Heat the water and oil in a skillet. Add the saffron, seasonings and artichokes. Arrange orange slices over the artichokes. Cover and simmer for 35 minutes.

Serve warm on a platter as a side dish.

Jazar mah Assal

Egypt

Honey-Glazed Carrots

Serves 6

Glazed carrots are popular in African and Middle Eastern cuisine. They complement any meal.

12	**small carrots**	12
	water and pinch of salt	
⅓ cup	**honey**	75 mL
2 tbsp.	**olive or vegetable oil**	30 mL
1 tsp.	**lemon juice**	5 mL
½ tsp.	**salt**	2 mL

Combine carrots and water to cover with a pinch of salt in a saucepan. Bring to a boil. Reduce heat, cover and cook until tender, approximately 12 minutes. Drain and set aside.

Combine all remaining ingredients in a large skillet, cook uncovered over medium heat until bubbly. Add carrots and cook uncovered over low heat, occasionally stirring gently, for 2-3 minutes until carrots are glazed.

Cebollas al Horno

Baked Onions

Serves 4

Onions are a favorite dish of most Spaniards. This recipe from Murcia which uses sweet Spanish onions is a delicious way to serve them.

8	large Spanish onions, peeled	8
6	garlic cloves, minced	6
4 tbsp.	olive oil	60 mL
2 tbsp.	dry white wine	30 mL
½	lemon, juice of	½
½ tsp.	salt	2 mL
	freshly ground pepper	
1 tbsp.	paprika	15 mL
2 tbsp.	chopped parsley	30 mL

Heat oven to 325°F (160°C).

Place onions in a well-greased, shallow, ovenproof dish and sprinkle with garlic.

Blend together the oil, wine, lemon juice, salt, pepper and paprika and pour over the onions. Sprinkle with parsley.

Cover the dish with foil and cook for 1½ hours, or until onions are tender.

Serve as a side dish.

Basal Makala

Egypt

Three Onion Sauté

Serves 4-6

¼ cup	olive oil	60 mL
2	medium red onions, cut into ¼" (1 cm) slices	2
2 cups	green onions, chopped into 2" (5 cm) pieces	500 mL
2	medium onions, cut into ¼" (1 cm) slices	2
½ cup	vegetable stock (page 72) or water	125 mL
2 tbsp.	lemon juice	30 mL
2 tbsp.	sugar	30 mL
⅛ tsp.	coriander	0.5 mL
	salt and pepper to taste	

Heat oil in a heavy skillet over medium heat. Add all the onions. Cover and cook for 10 minutes, stirring occasionally. Uncover and cook for approximately 10 minutes more, stirring occasionally. Add all remaining ingredients. Cook for 5 minutes, stirring occasionally.

Serve warm with stews or a sandwich.

Bitinjan Mishwi

Grilled Eggplant   Serves 4

Such a simple recipe, but in great demand at The Cedars Restaurant.

2	large eggplants	2
¼ cup	olive or vegetable oil	60 mL
1 tbsp.	oregano	15 mL
1 tsp.	salt	5 mL
½ tsp.	pepper	2 mL

Wash eggplants. Do not peel. Remove stem, slice lengthwise in ½" (1.3 cm) slices. Brush oil on each side, sprinkle remaining ingredients evenly over all.

Grill each side on barbecue over medium-hot coals, or under broiler. Eggplant should be soft and lightly golden.

Serve with a spoonful of yogurt, sour cream or Tzatziki (page 24).

VARIATION:
Replace eggplant with zucchini and follow the same directions.

See photograph on page 88.

Ijjit Koosa mah Batata

Zucchini Potato Cake

Lebanon

Serves 4

2	medium zucchini, grated	2
1	large potato, grated	1
4	eggs	4
3 tbsp.	flour	45 mL
1 tsp.	salt	5 mL
½ tsp.	pepper	2 mL
½ cup	finely chopped green onions	125 mL
½ cup	finely chopped parsley	125 mL
1 ½ cups	oil, for frying	375 mL

Rinse the grated zucchini and potato. Using both hands, squeeze out all the water. Place in a mixing bowl. Add remaining ingredients, except oil, and mix (do not beat).

Heat oil for frying. Using a large tablespoon (15 mL), drop mixture into hot oil, getting as many patties as possible in the frying pan at a time. Turn over when one side is golden brown and cook the other side. Remove from oil and drain on paper towels.

These mini omelettes can be served with pickles, inside pita bread.

Batata bi Limoon

Lemon Potatoes

Lebanon

Serves 4

A side dish that goes well with any meal. Potatoes are flavored with lemon and herbs.

4	medium potatoes, peeled and sliced crosswise	4
4 tbsp.	olive oil	60 mL
¼ cup	lemon juice	60 mL
½ tsp.	salt	2 mL
½ tsp.	pepper	2 mL
2	garlic cloves, minced	2
½ tsp.	rosemary	2 mL
½ tsp.	oregano	2 mL
¼ tsp.	paprika	1 mL

Place first 6 ingredients in a large mixing bowl. Toss well. Place potatoes and marinade on a baking sheet, spreading evenly. Combine herbs and paprika and sprinkle over potatoes. Grill under broiler until golden brown, approximately 10 minutes. Turn over and grill other side.

Serve hot or cold with the lemony juices.

Pommes Parisiennes

France

Parisienne Potatoes

Serves 4

2 tbsp.	butter	30 mL
2 tbsp.	olive oil	30 mL
1½ lbs.	small new potatoes (scrape only bruised skin)	750 g
1 tsp.	salt	5 mL
½ tsp.	white pepper	2 mL
4 tbsp.	softened butter	60 mL
2 tbsp.	finely chopped basil	30 mL
2 tbsp.	finely chopped coriander	30 mL
	basil and coriander sprigs for garnish	

Heat butter and oil in a large heavy frying pan over medium heat. Pat potatoes dry. Add them to the oil. Stir to coat evenly with the oil. Fry until lightly browned, approximately 20 minutes. Reduce heat. Sprinkle with salt and pepper; cover and cook for 12-15 minutes, shaking pan frequently until potatoes are tender. Turn heat to high, shake pan until potatoes start to sizzle. Remove from heat. Add the butter and herbs.

Serve as a side dish on a warm platter. Garnish with basil and coriander sprigs.

Potato Tortillas

Spain

Serves 4

4	medium potatoes	4
4	eggs	4
	vegetable oil for frying	
	olive oil	
½ tsp.	salt	2 mL

Peel potatoes and cut them into ⅛" (3 mm) slices. In a frying pan, add vegetable oil to a depth of approximately ¼" (1 cm). Heat oil over medium heat. Fry the potato slices, a few at a time, until soft but not browned. Color should be pale. Drain on paper towels.

Beat eggs in mixing bowl. Add potato slices. Mix to coat. Heat a thin coating of olive oil in a heavy frying pan over medium heat. Add one-quarter of the potato and egg mixture, shape should resemble a pancake. Fry until golden brown on each side.

Keep fried tortillas warm in the oven until all the potatoes are fried.

Sprinkle with salt.

Pipérade Basque

Scrambled Eggs with Vegetables

France

Serves 4

Eaten in the Basque country, this is a delightful way to serve eggs.

¼ cup	butter	60 mL
1	red pepper, seeded and thinly sliced	1
1	green pepper, seeded and thinly sliced	1
1	large onion, thinly sliced	1
1	garlic clove, minced	1
4	large tomatoes, skinned and chopped	4
½ tsp.	salt	2 mL
¼ tsp.	pepper	1 mL
6	eggs	6
¼ cup	milk	60 mL

Melt butter in a large frying pan. Add the peppers and fry over medium heat for approximately 5 minutes. Add the onion, garlic and tomatoes, continue cooking for 3 minutes. Add seasonings.

Beat eggs lightly with a fork. Add milk. Pour over the vegetables.

Reduce heat, cook gently, stirring until eggs are set and creamy. Turn out onto heated plates.

Serve hot with bread as a starter or light lunch.

Fool mah Bayd

Lebanon

Fava Beans with Eggs

Serves 4

Green broad beans or fava beans can be purchased from supermarkets canned, frozen, or fresh from the garden using the beans inside the pod. Whole tender green beans with the pod can be substituted. String and cut beans into 1½" (4 cm) lengths.

1	**medium onion, coarsely chopped**	1
¼ cup	**butter**	60 mL
4 cups	**green broad beans (fava beans)**	1 L
¼ cup	**water**	60 mL
½ tsp.	**cumin**	2 mL
1 tsp.	**salt**	5 mL
¼ tsp.	**pepper**	1 mL
4	**eggs**	4

Sauté onions in butter until onions are limp. Add beans and stir; fry for 2 minutes on medium heat.

Add water and cover with lid. Cook over medium-low heat for 20-25 minutes, until beans are tender.

Add seasonings. Break eggs and add to bean mixture, stirring slightly to break the yolk. Cook only until eggs are set.

Serve with pita bread, sliced tomatoes or Yogurt Cucumber Salad (page 29).

Champinones al Ajillo

Spain

Mushrooms with Garlic

Serves 4

A side dish with mushrooms and garlic. Very quick to prepare.

2 tbsp.	olive or vegetable oil	30 mL
6	garlic cloves, finely chopped	6
8 oz.	mushrooms, halved	250 g
2 tbsp.	dry sherry	30 mL
1 tsp.	lemon juice	5 mL
¼ tsp.	salt	1 mL
¼ tsp.	pepper	1 mL
2 tbsp.	coarsely chopped parsley	30 mL

Heat oil in a large skillet until hot. Add garlic and cook over medium heat for 1 minute. Add mushrooms. Cook, stirring, for 2 minutes. Reduce heat, stir in remaining ingredients except parsley. Cook and stir for about 2 minutes. Remove from heat. Place in a serving dish, sprinkle with parsley.

Funghi Peperoni

Italy

Mushroom and Pepper Sauté

Serves 6

Easy to prepare, this is a colorful side dish.

¼ cup	butter	60 mL
2	small red bell peppers, cut into bite-sized pieces	2
2	small orange bell peppers, cut into bite-sized pieces	2
8 oz.	mushrooms, cut large mushrooms into smaller pieces	250 g
	salt and pepper to taste	
3 tbsp.	fresh tarragon leaves or 1½ tsp. (7 mL) dry	45 mL
½ tsp.	cumin	2 mL
¼ cup	crumbled feta cheese	60 mL

Melt butter in a large heavy skillet over medium heat. Add bell peppers and sauté until tender, about 5 minutes. Stir in mushrooms. Season to taste with salt and pepper. Sauté until mushrooms are golden brown, about 5 minutes. Mix in tarragon and cumin; cook 1 minute. Sprinkle with feta cheese. Stir gently and serve.

See photograph on page 69.

Fleifleh Mishwi

Egypt

Roasted Peppers

Serves 6

When the barbecue is on, try roasting these peppers for the side dish.

| 6 | **large sweet peppers, any color or mix colors** | 6 |

Slice peppers in half, remove seeds. Roast over medium-hot coals on barbecue or under broiler until blackened. Rub off the charred skin with a paper towel. Slice peppers into thin strips. Serve on a platter garnished with pieces of fresh cilantro or watercress.

DRESSING FOR ROASTED PEPPERS

1	**garlic clove, minced**	1
¼ cup	**olive oil**	60 mL
1 tbsp.	**chopped parsley**	15 mL
1 tbsp.	**chopped basil**	15 mL
¼ cup	**lemon juice**	60 mL
	salt and pepper to taste	

Mix all ingredients together in a small mixing bowl. Drizzle over the sliced peppers.

See photograph on page 156.

Green Pepper and Spinach

Turkey

Serves 4

Other vegetables may be added to this dish. Try it with celery or zucchini.

1	**medium onion, chopped**	1
1	**medium green pepper, chopped**	1
1 tbsp.	**olive or vegetable oil**	15 mL
1	**large tomato, chopped**	1
1 lb.	**fresh spinach**	500 g
½ tsp.	**salt or to taste**	2 mL
¼ tsp.	**pepper**	1 mL
¼ cup	**peanut butter**	60 mL

Combine onion, pepper and oil in a 3-quart (3 L) saucepan. Cook until onion is tender. Add tomato and spinach. Cover and simmer for approximately 5 minutes, until spinach is tender. Stir in salt, pepper and peanut butter. Heat until just hot. Serve in serving bowl, cold or hot.

Sabanikh Mtabbel

Lebanon

Spinach with Lemon

Serves 2-3

1 lb.	fresh spinach	500 g
4 tbsp.	butter	60 mL
½	onion, finely diced	½
1	garlic clove, crushed	1
1½ tsp.	salt	7 mL
½ tsp.	pepper	2 mL
¼ tsp.	coriander	1 mL
½	lemon, juice of	½

Wash spinach well, and chop into large pieces. Set aside. Melt butter in a large saucepan, add diced onion and garlic. Sauté until onion is limp. Add spinach and seasonings. Cook over medium heat until spinach has wilted, occasionally turning over the spinach with a wooden spoon. Remove from heat. Squeeze lemon juice over spinach mixture.

Serve on top of Rice Pilaf (page 85).

Spanaki Pilafi

Greece

Spinach Pilaf

Serves 4

1 lb.	spinach, washed well and drained	500 g
¾ cup	rice, rinsed and drained	175 mL
	water	
1 tsp.	salt	5 mL
¼ tsp.	pepper	1 mL
¼ tsp.	mint	1 mL
½ cup	olive oil	125 mL
1	fresh lemon, halved	1

Place spinach in a saucepan. Simmer over low heat, covered, for 10 minutes. Set aside.

Place rice in a 2-quart (2 L) saucepan, add enough water to cover. Bring to a boil, stir rice with a fork, then simmer until water is absorbed.

Add the partially cooked rice to the spinach, stir carefully with a fork to mix. Add salt, pepper and mint. Cover and simmer on low heat for 10-15 minutes, until rice is fully cooked.

In a frying pan, heat olive oil to the sizzling point. Do not allow to burn. Pour hot oil over the rice and spinach, stirring carefully to mix. Cover pot. Let sit for 10 minutes before serving.

Serve in a shallow bowl and squeeze plenty of lemon juice over Pilaf.

Kritharaki me Rize

Greek Orzo and Rice Pilaf

Greece

Serves 2-3

This pilaf is served with almost every meal, especially stewed dishes. Orzo is a pasta made in the shape of rice.

½ cup	orzo	125 mL
3 tbsp.	butter	45 mL
⅔ cup	rice, rinsed and drained	150 mL
3 cups	vegetable stock (page 72) or water	750 mL
	grated kefalotiri cheese (optional)	

Sauté orzo in butter in a medium-sized saucepan, until lightly brown. Add rice, stir to coat with the butter. Add stock. Bring to a boil. Reduce heat to simmer, cover and cook for 25 minutes. Serve on a platter with grated kefalotiri cheese if desired.

Ruz M'Falfal

Rice Pilaf

Lebanon

Serves 4

This Pilaf goes hand in hand with any stewed dishes.

½ cup	vermicelli or fine egg noodles, broken into 1-2" (2.5-3 cm) pieces	125 mL
¼ cup	unsalted butter	60 mL
1½ cups	rice, soaked in hot water for 1 hour	375 mL
1 tsp.	salt	5 mL
2½ cups	water	625 mL

Brown noodles in butter in a saucepan over medium heat. Add drained rice, stirring over high heat for 1 minute. Stir in salt and water. Bring to a boil. Turn heat to low, simmer, covered, for 20-25 minutes, or until rice is tender.

NOTE:

If rice is not presoaked, wash and drain rice. Add an additional ½ cup (125 mL) water to above. Cooking time will be 5-10 minutes longer.

Lebanon

This tiny country bordered by Syria, Israel and the Mediterranean Sea is the country where I was born. People are very hospitable and generous and the more a guest eats, the more he shows his love and affection for his host. This is where people take much pride in their cuisine and compete to make the most superior tabouli, hommous or falafel. In Lebanon, a formal meal is transformed into a huge buffet with dozens of dishes prepared with the utmost pride and care.

Lebanese cuisine is never overpowering and is very pleasing to the palate. Breakfast is light with yogurt, olives and cheese. Lunch is a larger meal that might be served between 2-3 p.m. Dinner is enjoyed early in the evening and is a lighter meal.

The Lebanese cultivate an abundance of grains, vegetables and fruits. Many olive and mulberry trees are found in the lush and fertile valleys. Yogurt and olives are staples on every table. Bulgar, chickpeas, beans, lentils, rice, olive oil and tahini are ingredients which are necessities to every cook. Eggplant, zucchini and tomatoes, seasoned with herbs, garlic and spices, are used in stews or are hollowed out and stuffed to create wonderful gourmet dishes. Cinnamon is sprinkled on rice dishes, allspice and cloves are used in desserts. Basil is often added liberally to vegetable dishes and lemon juice is a frequent addition to recipes.

Arak, an anise-flavored liqueur is sometimes served with meals. This is similar to the Greek Ouzo. Lebanon also produces great wines. Alcohol is consumed in moderation. It is not customary to always drink with meals.

There are many similarities among the cuisines of the bordering countries. As neighbors do, they borrow cuisines and customs from each other. Lebanese chefs are in great demand in other Arab countries. They are well respected for their expertise and creativity in the preparation of this wonderful and healthy cuisine. The Lebanese create amazing gourmet dishes with inexpensive ingredients.

Lebanese cuisine has become very popular on the Western cooking scene. The extraordinary culinary uses of beans, peas and vegetables provide exotic flavors and scents to the impressive dishes of this magnificent country.

Photograph Opposite

Top — *Salatat Khodra (Layered Salad), page 30*
Center Left — *Bitinjan Mah Fyllo (Eggplant Fyllo Layer), page 131*
Center Right — *Baklawa (Baklava), page 150*
Bottom — *Kmaj Mahamas (Pita Chips), page 18*

Risotto e Ceci

Chickpea Risotto

Serves 6

An Italian risotto is more moist than the Spanish rice dishes. It's well worth making and has been around as long as pasta. Cooked slowly, stirred frequently and flavored with cheese, it has a wonderfully creamy texture.

6 tbsp.	butter	90 mL
1 cup	chopped onion	250 mL
2	fresh rosemary sprigs or 1½ tsp. (7 mL) dried	2
½ cup	finely chopped fennel or celery	125 mL
¼ cup	chopped parsley	60 mL
2 cups	cooked chickpeas	500 mL
1 tsp.	salt	5 mL
2½ cups	Arborio rice or any short-grain rice, rinsed and drained	625 mL
6 cups	vegetable stock (page 72)	1.5 L
⅔ cup	freshly grated Parmesan cheese	150 mL

Melt the butter in a large heavy saucepan over medium heat. Add the onions. Sauté until transparent. Stir in the rosemary and fennel or celery. Sauté for 3 minutes. Add the parsley, chickpeas and salt. Sauté for a further 3 minutes. Add the rice and sauté for 2-3 minutes, stirring constantly.

Add ½ cup (125 mL) of the stock. Reduce heat and simmer until liquid is absorbed, stirring frequently. Continue adding stock, ½ cup (125 mL) at a time, stirring frequently and allowing each addition of the stock to be absorbed before the next addition, for approximately 30 minutes. After last addition of stock, stir and cover for 5 minutes. Rice should be tender and sticky.

Remove risotto from heat. Add the Parmesan cheese, mix gently and serve.

NOTE:
Arborio rice is an Italian short-grain rice recommended for this recipe and available at Italian markets or specialty food stores.

Photograph Opposite

Top — ***Bitinjan Mishwi (Grilled Eggplant), page 77***
Centre — ***Zonkol bi Laban (Bulgar Balls in Cold Yogurt), page 54***
Bottom — ***Saffi, page 41***

Shier M'Falfal

Barley Pilaf Casserole

This simple pilaf with barley and mushrooms has a delicious nutty texture.

2 tbsp.	butter	30 mL
¼ cup	olive oil	60 mL
2 cups	finely chopped onions	500 mL
2 cups	sliced mushrooms	500 mL
1 cup	diced celery	250 mL
1½ cups	uncooked pot barley	375 mL
5 cups	vegetable stock (page 72) or water	1.25 L
1 tsp.	salt	5 mL
½ tsp.	pepper	2 mL

Set oven to 375°F (190°C).

Melt butter in a large heavy skillet, add oil, then onions. Cook over medium heat for 5 minutes. Add mushrooms and celery. Cook for 3 minutes over low heat stirring occasionally.

Transfer vegetables to a bowl and set aside.

Add barley to the skillet. Cook over low heat, stirring often, until well-browned, for approximately 10 minutes.

Place barley into a 2-quart (2 L) casserole. Stir in vegetable stock and seasonings.

Cover and bake for 45 minutes. Add sautéed vegetables, stir, continue to bake for an additional 30 minutes.

Serve with a salad.

Burghul M'Falfal

Bulgar Pilaf

A change from rice, bulgar has really come a long way in popularity.

¼ cup	butter	60 mL
1½ cups	coarse bulgar (crushed wheat)	375 mL
1 tsp.	salt	5 mL
¼ tsp.	pepper	1 mL
3 cups	water	750 mL

Combine butter and bulgar in a saucepan. Sauté over medium heat for 1 minute. Stir in seasonings and add water. Bring to a boil. Turn heat to low, cover and simmer for 20-25 minutes.

Bulgar should be fluffy and moist. Delicious with cold yogurt.

Serve as a substitute for rice pilaf.

VARIATION:

After adding the water, place bulgar mixture in a casserole. Cover and bake in a 350°F (180°C) oven for 20 minutes. Stir gently and return to oven. Cover and bake for another 10 minutes.

Kmaj

Pita Bread

This bread adapts very well to any type of food. It is served with every Lebanese meal. Tear a bite-sized piece from the pita round and use it to pick up morsels of food from the plate.

2½ cups	lukewarm water	625 mL
1 tsp.	sugar	5 mL
3½ tsp.	active dry yeast	17 mL
1 tsp.	salt	5 mL
5½ cups	flour (white or whole-wheat)	1.4 L
	vegetable oil	

Place water and sugar in a large bowl and stir. Add yeast and stir slightly. Let rest for 5 minutes.

Mix in salt and flour gradually, starting with 3½ cups (875 mL) flour then adding the rest. More or less water may be required, depending on the brand of flour. Use enough flour to prevent dough from clinging to bowl. Knead well for 5 minutes. Place a little vegetable oil on palms of hands and smooth over all the dough to prevent crusting. Cover with plastic wrap then a tea towel and allow to rest for 20-30 minutes.

Set oven at 500°F (260°C).

Divide dough into 8 balls. Roll out each ball to ¼" (1 cm) thickness. Let rest, covered, for 20 minutes on generously floured table or counter top.

Bake on greased cookie sheets for 5-8 minutes, or until lightly browned. The higher the oven temperature the better the results. Due to the temperature in a domestic oven not reaching the high temperature of a commercial oven, some pitas may not open up.

Pita can be kept in a plastic bag in the refrigerator for several days or may be frozen.

To warm pita, place the round on a rack in the oven at 300°F (150°C) for 1-2 minutes.

NOTE:
1. Cut pita in half and fill the pockets to make a sandwich.
2. Toast pita in the oven, crumble into bite-sized pieces, toss in salads to replace croûtons.
3. Make Pita Chips (page 18).

Focaccia

Italian Flat Bread

Italy

Makes 1

This bread has become very popular in North America. Very flavorful, it is garnished with dried or fresh herbs, similar to Manaiesh, an Arabian flat bread.

2 tsp.	active dry yeast	10 mL
1 cup	warm water	250 mL
3 tbsp.	chopped fresh rosemary or 1½ tsp. (7 mL) dry	45 mL
3 tbsp.	olive oil	45 mL
2 tsp.	salt	10 mL
2½-3 cups	flour	625-750 mL
	olive oil (for greasing baking sheet)	
	coarsely ground pepper	

Dissolve yeast in warm water in a large mixing bowl. Stir in rosemary, 3 tbsp. (45 mL) oil, salt and enough of the flour to make the dough easy to handle. Turn dough onto a floured board. Knead until smooth and elastic, 5-8 minutes. Place in a greased bowl and turn the greased side of the dough up. Cover and let rise in a warm place until doubled, approximately 1 hour.

Heat oven to 450°F (230°C).

Punch down dough. Press the dough into a greased 12" (30 cm) pizza pan or baking sheet.

Press fingers into the dough, spreading the dough evenly to the sides of the pan. Brush with oil, sprinkle with pepper. Cover and let rise for 20 minutes. Brush with additional oil. Bake for 15-20 minutes, or until golden brown. Cut into squares or tear. Serve warm.

VARIATIONS:
1. Before baking, add thinly sliced tomatoes, fresh basil, oregano or rosemary leaves and pitted black olives and press into the dough.
2. Add oats or whole-wheat flour to add fibre to the dough.

NOTE:
Using a food processor will cut preparation time.

See photograph on page 69.

Simit

Turkish Bread Rings

These sesame rings are displayed on sticks and sold by street vendors.

2 tbsp.	active dry yeast (2 env.)	30 mL
1½ cups	warm water	375 mL
1½ cups	milk, scalded, then cooled to lukewarm	375 mL
2 tbsp.	sugar	30 mL
1 tbsp.	salt	15 mL
2 tbsp.	vegetable oil or butter	30 mL
6½-7 cups	flour	1.6-1.75 L
	vegetable oil (for greasing bowl)	
2	eggs	2
¾ cup	sesame seeds	175 mL

Heat oven to 400°F (200°C).

Dissolve yeast in warm water in a large bowl. Stir in milk, sugar, salt, oil and 3 cups (750 mL) of the flour. Beat until smooth. Stir in enough of the remaining flour to make dough easy to handle. Turn dough onto floured surface and knead until smooth and elastic, for approximately 5 minutes. Grease a large bowl with the oil. Place dough in bowl and turn greased side of dough up. Cover, set in a warm place to rise until doubled, approximately 45-60 minutes.

Punch down dough, divide into 8-10 equal parts. Roll and shape each into a rope, about 12" (30 cm) long. Dampen ends with a little water, bring ends together, pinch to hold together forming a ring. Beat eggs with a fork. Spread sesame seeds on a large plate. Brush each ring with the egg. Dip the ring into the sesame seeds, pressing lightly. Place rings sesame side up on large greased baking sheets. Cover loosely and let rise until doubled, approximately 30 minutes. Remaining rings can be left on floured surface and when ready to bake transferred onto baking sheets.

Bake until golden brown, approximately 18-20 minutes.

Turkey

Makes 8-10

Main Courses

Vegetable Kabobs

Perfect at any backyard barbecue, served with a pilaf and garlic bread. For best results, vegetables should marinate for more than 2 hours, or even overnight.

1	**small eggplant about ¾ lb. (365 g), cut into 2" (5 cm) cubes**	1
3	**medium carrots, cut into ½" (1.3 cm) slices**	3
8	**small red potatoes, about 2-3" (5-7 cm) in diameter**	8
3	**medium zucchini, sliced lengthwise, then into 1" (2.5 cm) slices**	3
1	**large red or green bell pepper, seeded and cut into 1" (2.5 cm) squares**	1
2	**medium onions, cut in wedges (separate wedges into 2-3 layers each)**	2
16	**whole mushrooms**	16
	Herb Marinade (recipe page 97)	
	salt and pepper to taste	

Cook eggplant in 1" (2.5 cm) boiling water for 3 minutes and drain. Cook carrots in 1" (2.5 cm) boiling water until just tender crisp and drain. Cook unpeeled potatoes in 1" (2.5 cm) boiling water for approximately 15-20 minutes. Drain and cut in half.

Place eggplant, carrots, potatoes, zucchini, peppers, onions and mushrooms in a large plastic bag. Add marinade, seal bag well. Refrigerate for 2 hours or overnight.

Drain vegetables and reserve marinade.

Using 8 metal skewers, thread vegetables, alternating varieties. Place on lightly greased grill, over low heat. Cook, turning often, basting with the reserved marinade for 10-15 minutes, or until vegetables are tender. Sprinkle lightly with salt before serving. Remaining marinade can be used again. It can be refrigerated for up to 2 weeks.

Makes 8 skewers; 2 skewers per person.

NOTE:
If wooden skewers are used, soak them in water for 15-20 minutes before using. This prevents the wood from burning.

See photograph on page 51.

Herb Marinade for Vegetable Kebobs

Greece

Makes about 1 cup (250 mL)

¾ cup	olive oil	175 mL
¼ cup	white vinegar or lemon juice	60 mL
2	garlic cloves, minced	2
1 tsp.	Dijon mustard	5 mL
½ tsp.	basil	2 mL
½ tsp.	oregano	2 mL
½ tsp.	marjoram	2 mL
½ tsp.	rosemary	2 mL
¼ tsp.	pepper	1 mL

Combine all ingredients in a bowl and mix well.

Ardishowki Mah Lubi

Egypt

Artichoke and Green Bean Casserole

Serves 4

2 tbsp.	butter	30 mL
¼ cup	water	60 mL
½ tsp.	salt or to taste	2 mL
¼ tsp.	pepper	1 mL
2	garlic cloves, chopped	2
9 oz.	fresh or frozen artichoke hearts	255 g
9 oz.	fresh or frozen cut green beans	255 g
¼ cup	grated Parmesan cheese	60 mL

Set oven at 400°F (200°C).

Melt butter in a large saucepan. Stir in water, salt, pepper and garlic. Add the artichokes and beans. Stir and turn into a 1½-quart (1.5 L) casserole. Cover and bake for 1 hour, or until vegetables are tender, stirring once.

Remove casserole from oven, sprinkle cheese over vegetables. Cover, let stand 5 minutes before serving.

Anginares me Kefalotiri

Artichokes with Kefalotiri Sauce

Greece

Serves 6

2 cups	water	500 mL
¼ cup	lemon juice	60 mL
1½ lbs.	frozen artichoke hearts	750 g
½ cup	melted butter	125 mL
	salt and pepper to taste	
1	recipe Béchamel Sauce (below)	1
2 cups	grated kefalotiri cheese	500 mL
3-4 tbsp.	toasted bread crumbs	45-60 mL

Heat oven to 350°F (180°C).

Bring water to a boil in a 1-quart (1 L) saucepan. Add lemon juice and artichokes and cook for 5-7 minutes. Drain artichokes and cut into quarters. Pour ½ of the melted butter over and season. Prepare the Béchamel Sauce.

Butter a 7 x 9" (18 x 23 cm) baking dish. Spread a thin layer of the sauce in the dish. Sprinkle ⅓ of the cheese on top of the sauce. Spread the artichokes evenly and sprinkle another ⅓ of the cheese over them. Spoon remaining sauce all over. Top with remaining cheese and bread crumbs. Drizzle remaining butter over the bread crumbs.

Bake for 30 minutes, or until golden brown.

Béchamel Sauce

For Artichokes with Kefalotiri Sauce (above)

Greece

This is one of the favorite sauces in Greek cuisine.

6 tbsp.	butter	90 mL
8 tbsp.	flour	120 mL
3½ cups	hot milk	875 mL
2	egg yolks, slightly beaten	2
	salt and pepper to taste	

Melt the butter in a 2-quart (2 L) saucepan. Add the flour, blend well, lower heat. Add the hot milk, stirring rapidly with a wooden spoon or whisk, until the sauce thickens. Remove from heat and add egg yolks and seasonings. Stir well.

Cauolfiori e Finocchi Alla Panna

Cauliflower and Fennel in Cream

1	cauliflower, approximately 2½ lbs. (1.25 kg)	1
8 cups	boiling water	2 L
1 tsp.	salt	5 mL
4	fennel bulbs	4
1 tbsp.	flour	15 mL
1	large onion, chopped	1
¼ cup	butter	60 mL
1 cup	heavy cream	250 mL
	salt and pepper to taste	
1 cup	grated Parmesan cheese or grated Cheddar	250 mL

Heat oven to 350°F (180°C).

Separate the cauliflower into florets and wash well. Drop into boiling salted water. Cook for 3-4 minutes. Remove from water with a slotted spoon and place in a bowl, set aside. Reserve the water.

Remove the outer leaves of the fennel and discard. Cut fennel into wedges and drop into the boiling water; add the flour and stir while cooking. Cook until just tender. Drain.

Cook onion in butter in a large saucepan until golden brown. Add the cauliflower and fennel; brown lightly. Arrange in a 3-quart (3 L) baking dish. Cover with cream, add salt and pepper to taste.

Bake for 20 minutes, or until cream thickens. Sprinkle with Parmesan cheese or grated Cheddar.

Brown under broiler for a few minutes.

Serve hot.

Khodra bi Furn

Vegetable Mashed Potato Casserole

The Lebanese make a dish similar to this with ground meat and mashed potatoes. Although this version is vegetarian, it's just as flavorful and filling.

2	large potatoes, boiled in their skins	2
1½ tbsp.	butter	22 mL
	salt and pepper to taste	
½ cup	yogurt	125 mL
½ cup	finely chopped green onions	125 mL
¼ cup	finely chopped parsley	60 mL
2 tbsp.	butter or olive oil	30 mL
1 cup	chopped onions	250 mL
2	garlic cloves, minced	2
½ cup	bulgar	125 mL
1 tsp.	salt	5 mL
½ tsp.	pepper	2 mL
½ cup	finely chopped celery	125 mL
½ cup	sliced mushrooms	125 mL
1	medium eggplant, cut in small cubes	1
1	green pepper, finely chopped	1
½ tsp.	thyme	2 mL
½ tsp.	basil	2 mL
½ tsp.	oregano	2 mL
1 cup	peas, fresh or frozen	250 mL

Heat oven to 350°F (180°C).

Peel potatoes after they are cooked. Mash them with the next 5 ingredients. Set aside.

In a large skillet, sauté butter, onions, garlic, bulgar, salt and pepper over medium heat. Sauté until onions are transparent. Add celery, mushrooms and eggplant. Cover and cook over low heat, stirring occasionally until eggplant is just soft. Add the green pepper, herbs and peas. Continue to cook for 5 more minutes.

Remove from heat, place this mixture into a deep 3-quart (3 L) casserole. Spread the mashed potatoes on top. Bake for 40-45 minutes.

Serve hot with a salad.

Courgette Arlesienne

Zucchini Sauté

1	green pepper, diced	1
1	garlic clove, peeled and chopped	1
½ cup	finely chopped onion	125 mL
2 tbsp.	olive oil	30 mL
2	large zucchini	2
2	large tomatoes, diced	2
1 tsp.	salt	5 mL
½ tsp.	oregano	2 mL
1 tbsp.	capers	15 mL
1 tbsp.	pimientos	15 mL
1 tbsp.	sliced stuffed olives	15 mL

On medium heat, sauté the pepper, garlic and onion in oil in a large skillet. Cook for 5 minutes.

Wash and dice zucchini. Add zucchini, tomatoes and salt to the sautéed vegetables. Cover, cook slowly for 15 minutes. Add pepper, oregano and capers.

Increase the heat slightly, cook uncovered until almost all liquid has evaporated. Cool slightly and turn onto a deep serving platter.

Garnish with strips of pimiento and olives.

Serve chilled with a salad.

See photograph on page 34.

Koosa Bi Furn

Zucchini Casserole

2 tbsp.	olive oil	30 mL
2	medium zucchini, cubed	2
2	medium onions, cubed	2
2	green peppers, cubed	2
3	garlic cloves, crushed	3
¼ tsp.	thyme	1 mL
1	carrot, thinly sliced	1
2	cooked potatoes, cubed	2
2 cups	crushed tomatoes	500 mL
½ tsp.	cinnamon	2 mL
	salt and pepper to taste	
1 cup	ricotta cheese	250 mL

Set oven at 350°F (180°C).

Sauté first 7 ingredients in a large saucepan for 5-8 minutes.

Stir in potatoes, crushed tomatoes, cinnamon, salt and pepper. Pour into a 3-quart (3 L) casserole. Spread ricotta cheese on top. Bake for 30 minutes, until hot and bubbly.

Delicious served over Bulgar Pilaf (page 91).

Kolokithákia Me Feta

Zucchini with Feta

4	large zucchini	4
2 tbsp.	salt	30 mL
½ cup	flour or as much as required	125 mL
½ cup	grated Parmesan cheese	125 mL
2 tbsp.	finely chopped fresh mint or 1 tsp. (5 mL) dry	30 mL
1 cup	crumbled feta cheese	250 mL
½ cup	shredded mozzarella cheese	125 mL
½ cup	olive or vegetable oil	125 mL

Heat oven to 400°F (200°C).

Slice zucchini lengthwise into ½" (1.3 cm) thick slices. Sprinkle with salt, place in a colander and let stand until water drains, approximately 2 hours.

Rinse zucchini and squeeze dry with paper towels. Coat each zucchini slice with flour. Place a layer of zucchini in a 9" (22 cm) square greased baking pan.

Sprinkle with ⅓ of the Parmesan cheese, mint and feta. Repeat layers of zucchini, cheeses and mint but save enough zucchini for a top layer. Sprinkle mozzarella over all. Top with a layer of zucchini. Pour oil over all. Bake for 45 minutes, or until the zucchini is tender. Cool for 25-30 minutes. Cut into squares.

Serve hot or at room temperature. Serve with a salad.

Quiche de Courgette

Zucchini Quiche

This quiche is absolutely magnifique. Slice into thin wedges for appetizers or thick wedges for a main course.

1	9" (23 cm) pastry shell, (page 152)	1
1	egg, slightly beaten	1
1 cup	shredded zucchini	250 mL
½ cup	minced onion	125 mL
1 tbsp.	butter	15 mL
1 cup	shredded Swiss cheese	250 mL
3	eggs	3
1½ cups	whipping cream	375 mL
¾ tsp.	salt	3 mL
¼ tsp.	white pepper	1 mL
¼ tsp.	nutmeg	1 mL

Preheat oven to 375°F (190°C).

Prepare pie shell and brush bottom with beaten egg; set aside. Using your hands, squeeze the liquid out of the zucchini. Discard liquid.

Sauté onions in butter until transparent. Arrange onions and zucchini on bottom of pie shell. Sprinkle the cheese evenly over the vegetables and set aside.

Beat together all remaining ingredients. Pour into pie shell. Bake in center of oven for 1 hour.

Serve hot or cold.

See photograph on page 33.

Tortilla Espanola

Spanish Omelette

A Spanish omelette is not like the French one at all. It's heavier and the shape is round. This is a basic recipe.

¼ cup	olive oil	60 mL
2	large potatoes, finely diced, about 2 cups (500 mL)	2
1	medium onion, finely diced	1
½ tsp.	salt	2 mL
¼ tsp.	pepper	1 mL
4	eggs, beaten	4

Heat a nonstick pan over medium heat, add oil. Add the potatoes and onions, sprinkle with seasonings. Cover and cook slowly for 10 minutes, until tender, stirring occasionally to prevent sticking.

Remove vegetables from pan, combine in a mixing bowl with the beaten eggs.

Wipe frying pan clean. Add just enough oil to cover the bottom of the pan. Heat pan on low to medium heat. Pour in the vegetable mixture. Spread evenly to the edges.

Cook, shaking pan to prevent sticking, until tortilla is firm and slides away from sides. Flip over and cook the other side or place a plate over the tortilla and flip pan over. Then slide tortilla back into the pan.

Slice and serve hot or cold for breakfast, lunch, dinner or snacks.

VARIATIONS:
1. Vegetables such as asparagus, peppers and mushrooms can be added to the potatoes and onions.
2. To make small omelettes: divide batter into 4 portions and cook each omelette separately.

French Omelette

Dress up this omelette with any of the fillings below. It makes a hearty meal.

2	**eggs**	**2**
1 tbsp.	**water**	**15 mL**
	pinch of salt	
	dash of pepper	
1 tbsp.	**butter or olive oil**	**15 mL**

If you intend to use one of the fillings below, prepare the filling first.

Break eggs into a bowl, beat with a fork. Add water and seasonings, beat again. Heat a small frying pan (pan is hot enough when a drop of water will roll around instead of bursting into steam). Heat oil or butter, coating the pan. Pour egg mixture into pan. Stir with prongs of fork, pushing the cooked portions from the bottom of pan (this will resemble scrambled eggs). Before eggs are cooked and are still creamy, spread evenly in pan. Top ½ of the omelette with filling. Slip a spatula under the unfilled side of the omelette and fold it over the filling. Slide onto a warm plate.

VARIATIONS:
1. Mushroom and Cheese Omelette: Add sliced mushrooms and shredded cheese.
2. Herb Omelette: Add a pinch each of basil, thyme and sage to eggs before cooking.
3. Ratatouille Omelette: Fill with Ratatouille (page 126).
4. Pepper and Tomato Omelette: Combine ½ cup (125 mL) of diced green pepper and 1 tomato, seeded and chopped, and fold into the omelette.

Oeufs à la Florentine

Eggs Florentine

Try this dish for breakfast or lunch. À la Florentine means a dish contains spinach. Superb with the wonderful Mornay Sauce.

10 oz.	fresh spinach, chopped	285 g
	Mornay Sauce (recipe below)	
4	poached eggs (recipe below)	4
2 tbsp.	grated Parmesan cheese	30 mL
1 tbsp.	dry bread crumbs	15 mL

Cook spinach in boiling water for 5 minutes. Drain and place in an ungreased 1-quart (1 L) baking dish. Keep warm. Prepare Mornay Sauce and poached eggs. Place eggs on top of spinach. Cover with Mornay Sauce. Sprinkle with the cheese and bread crumbs.

Broil about 6" (15 cm) from the top of the oven until lightly browned, approximately 1 minute.

MORNAY SAUCE FOR EGGS FLORENTINE

2 tsp.	butter	10 mL
2 tsp.	flour	10 mL
½ tsp.	salt	2 mL
¼ tsp.	nutmeg	1 mL
¼ tsp.	cayenne pepper or to taste	1 mL
¾ cup	half and half (creamilk)	175 mL
¼ cup	shredded Swiss cheese	60 mL

Melt butter in a 1-quart (1 L) saucepan. Blend in flour, salt, nutmeg and cayenne pepper. Cook over low heat, stirring constantly until smooth and bubbly. Stir in half and half. Heat to boiling, stirring constantly. Simmer and continue stirring for 1 minute. Add cheese, stir until melted.

POACHED EGGS FOR EGGS FLORENTINE

Heat water, 2" (5 cm) deep, to boiling in a shallow pan. Reduce heat to simmer.

Break each egg into a saucer, slide gently into the water. Cook to desired texture, 3-5 minutes. Remove with slotted spoon.

Baked Eggs in Tomato Shells

France

Serves 4

Tomatoes and eggs garnished with watercress make a wonderful breakfast or lunch.

4	**medium tomatoes**	4
	salt and pepper to taste	
4 tsp.	**bread crumbs, toasted**	20 mL
4 tsp.	**finely chopped basil**	20 mL
4 tsp.	**butter**	20 mL
4	**large eggs**	4
2 tbsp.	**grated Parmesan cheese**	30 mL
4	**slices of bread, toasted and buttered**	4
	watercress	

Preheat oven to 350°F (180°C).

Cut a thin slice from the top of each tomato. Remove all pulp and seeds to make a hollow shell. Discard pulp. Sprinkle the inside with salt. Turn tomatoes upside down and leave to drain. Sprinkle inside of tomatoes with salt and pepper to taste.

Combine the bread crumbs, basil and butter and divide equally among the tomato shells. Break 1 egg into each shell. Place tomatoes in a buttered baking dish. Bake for 20-25 minutes. Do not let tomatoes get too soft. Sprinkle with Parmesan cheese. Place under broiler to toast very lightly.

Serve on warm buttered toast and garnish with watercress.

Tomates à la Provençale

France

Stuffed Tomatoes

Serves 6

¼ cup	pine nuts	60 mL
3	large firm tomatoes	3
1 tsp.	salt	5 mL
½ tsp.	pepper	2 mL
½ tsp.	sugar	2 mL
2 tbsp.	olive oil	30 mL
¼ cup	finely chopped green onions	60 mL
1 cup	bread crumbs	250 mL
½ cup	pistou (recipe below)	125 mL

Set oven at 450°F (230°C).

Place pine nuts on cookie sheet. Toast in oven for 5 minutes until golden. Set aside.

Cut tomatoes in ½, widthwise. Remove seeds and pulp. Sprinkle evenly with the salt, pepper and sugar.

Heat oil in a small pan, add onions and sauté until wilted. Add the crumbs and pistou. Remove from heat and stir well.

Place tomato halves in a shallow baking dish.

Spoon the onion and crumb mixture evenly into the tomato halves.

Bake for 25 minutes.

Garnish with toasted pine nuts.

See photograph on page 34.

Pistou

France

Basil Sauce

Makes 1½ cups (375 mL)

Delicious served with all vegetable dishes.

2 cups	loosely packed, fresh basil leaves	500 mL
⅔ cup	chopped parsley	150 mL
¼ cup	pine nuts	60 mL
⅔ cup	olive oil	150 mL
4	garlic cloves, minced	4
⅓ cup	grated Parmesan cheese	75 mL
⅓ cup	Romano cheese	75 mL
2 tbsp.	soft butter	30 mL

Place all ingredients except cheeses and butter in processor or blender. Process until smooth.

Add cheeses and butter, process until thoroughly blended.

Fleifleh Mahshi

Bulgar-Stuffed Peppers

Egypt

Serves 8

8	large green peppers	8
½ cup	dry chickpeas, soaked overnight	125 mL
1½ cups	bulgar (crushed wheat)	375 mL
¾ cup	warm water	175 mL
¼ cup	chopped parsley	60 mL
½ cup	finely chopped green onion	125 mL
1½ tbsp.	fresh mint or 1¼ tsp. (6 mL) dry	22 mL
1 tsp.	salt	5 mL
½ tsp.	pepper	2 mL
¼ tsp.	coriander	1 mL
¼ tsp.	cinnamon	1 mL
¼ cup	vegetable oil	60 mL
2 cups	tomato sauce	500 mL
	hot water	

Remove stems and core peppers through a 1" (2.5 cm) opening at the stem end.

Drain chickpeas and place them on a tea towel. Roll chickpeas with a rolling pin to crack the skin. Place them in a mixing bowl with 3-4 cups (750 mL-1 L) water. Remove and discard the skins that float. Drain chickpeas and add all ingredients except the peppers, tomato sauce and hot water.

Set oven at 400°F (200°C). Stuff peppers to 1" (2.5 cm) below opening. Place side by side in a deep baking dish. Fill the peppers with some tomato sauce. Add the remaining sauce to the pan. Add enough water for the tomato sauce to reach halfway up the peppers.

Cover and bake approximately 45 minutes, then lower heat to 350°F (180°C). Cover and bake for another 30 minutes.

VARIATIONS:
1. This recipe is excellent for stuffing grape vine leaves, Swiss chard, eggplant, spinach, tomatoes, zucchini or cabbage. Stuff hollowed-out vegetables and follow the directions for cooking in this recipe. A few more or less chickpeas can be used or omit the chickpeas altogether.
2. This meatless stuffing is excellent served hot or cold, with fresh cold yogurt or salads.

Couscous Vegetarian Style

Morocco

Serves 8

2 tbsp.	olive oil	30 mL
4	small carrots, cut into 2" (5 cm) pieces	4
1	large onion, thickly sliced	1
2	garlic cloves, chopped	2
2 tsp.	chopped fresh coriander or 1 tsp. (5 mL) dry	10 mL
1½ tsp.	salt	7 mL
¼ tsp.	cayenne pepper	1 mL
¼ tsp.	turmeric	1 mL
1 cup	water or vegetable stock (page 72)	250 mL
3	medium zucchini, cut into ½" (1.3 cm) slices	3
2 cups	chickpeas (garbanzo beans), cooked and drained	500 mL
1⅓ cups	couscous	325 mL
	salt	
1¼ cups	boiling water	300 mL
½ cup	butter	125 mL
½ tsp.	ground turmeric	2 mL

Heat oil in a Dutch oven until hot. Add carrots and next 6 ingredients. Stir. Add water or vegetable stock. Bring to a boil. Reduce heat, cover and simmer for 20 minutes.

Add zucchini, cook for 10 minutes, until zucchini are tender, add chickpeas. Stir, remove from heat.

Combine couscous, salt and boiling water in a bowl. Set aside until water is absorbed, approximately 10 minutes.

Melt butter in a large skillet over medium heat. Stir in couscous and turmeric. Cook, stirring for 2 minutes.

Spread couscous on a large platter. Mound vegetables on top of the couscous or mix together.

To serve use pieces of French bread to pick up mouthfuls of couscous.

NOTE:
Fine bulgar wheat can be substituted for the couscous in this recipe.

See photograph on page 155.

Falafel

This vegetarian delight is the pride of the Middle East. It is frequently found in restaurants and delicatessens in the Middle East and now in North America.

1 lb.	dry chickpeas (do not use cooked chickpeas)	500 g
1	medium onion, quartered	1
1	medium potato, peeled, quartered	1
4	garlic cloves	4
1 tsp.	ground coriander	5 mL
1 tsp.	cumin	5 mL
2 tsp.	salt or to taste	10 mL
½ tsp.	pepper	2 mL
½ tsp.	cayenne or to taste	2 mL
1 tbsp.	flour	15 mL
	vegetable oil for frying	
½ tsp.	baking soda	2 mL
	Tahini, Sesame Seed Sauce (page 23)	

Soak chickpeas for 24 hours. Drain. Put chickpeas, onion, potato and garlic through meat grinder twice, using the finest grind, or chop in a food processor.

Add all remaining ingredients except vegetable oil, baking soda and Tahini. Mix well. Cover and let rest for 2-3 hours.

Heat oil for deep-frying. While oil is heating, add baking soda to the chickpea mixture. With dampened hands, form mixture into balls the size of walnuts, then flatten slightly into a patty or use a falafel mold*. Deep-fry, making sure patties are cooked through and are golden brown. Remove from oil with a slotted spoon and drain on paper towels.

Serve Falafel inside a round of pita bread. Open the bread around the outside edges of the round, leaving approximately 3" (7 cm) intact. Fill with 3 or 4 patties, sliced radishes, chopped parsley, diced tomatoes, pickle and hot peppers. Drizzle Sesame Seed Sauce over the vegetables. Cover filling with the top layer of the pita. Roll up pita, starting from 1 side. Or cut a small pita bread in ½ to form a pocket and fill. Small patties dipped into the Sesame Seed Sauce make a delightful appetizer.

VARIATION:
1. ½ lb. (250 g) dry fava beans or dry broad beans and ½ lb. (250 g) chickpeas can be used, following the same directions.

NOTE:
* Falafel molds are available at Middle Eastern shops.

See photograph on front cover.

Warak Dawali Mah Ruz

Lebanon

Grape Leaves Stuffed with Rice

Serves 6

Myles has these vine leaves almost everytime he comes to The Cedars Restaurant.

40-50	grape leaves, fresh or in brine	40-50
1½ cups	rice, rinsed and drained	375 mL
½ cup	finely chopped parsley	125 mL
2 tbsp.	chopped fresh mint or 1 tbsp. (15 mL) dry	30 mL
2	medium tomatoes, finely diced	2
½ cup	chopped green onions	125 mL
1 tsp.	salt	5 mL
½ tsp.	pepper	2 mL
½ tsp.	cinnamon	2 mL
¼ cup	vegetable oil	60 mL
¼ cup	lemon juice	60 mL

If using preserved grape leaves, drain off the brine and rinse the leaves in cold water several times. If fresh leaves are used, let stand in boiling water for 10 minutes to soften. Remove stems.

Combine all ingredients, except grape leaves, in a mixing bowl. Mix well. Place the grape leaf shiny side down. Place 1 tbsp. (15 mL) of the filling in a line in the center of the leaf. Fold the outside edges ½" (1.3 cm) towards the center, then roll with a slight firmness into the shape of a finger. Place in a 2-quart (2 L) saucepan, seam down, alternating directions of each layer.

When all leaves are rolled, add water to reach just below the last row rolled. Bring to a gentle boil, then lower heat. Cover and simmer for 1 hour, until leaves are tender.

Serve hot or cold with fresh yogurt or salad.

VARIATION:
This filling can be used for stuffing vegetables. Try it with Swiss chard leaves, cored zucchini, eggplant, tomatoes or peppers.

NOTE:
Grape leaves can be picked from a grape vine, but be careful not to pick the leaves that have white fluffy backs. Turn over the leaf and check first. Pick only the leaves near the tip of the vine. These will be more tender and shiny.

Stuffed Grape Leaves

Turkey

Grape Leaves Stuffed with Lentils and Bulgar

Serves 6

There are many variations for stuffing grape leaves. This filling can be used to stuff cabbage or any vegetable that can be wrapped or filled.

1 cup	lentils	250 mL
3 cups	water	750 mL
½ cup	coarse bulgar	125 mL
1 cup	hot water	250 mL
¼ cup	vegetable oil	60 mL
⅓ cup	pine nuts	75 mL
¼ cup	finely diced onion	60 mL
¼ cup	finely chopped fresh mint	60 mL
⅓ cup	lemon juice	75 mL
1 tsp.	salt	5 mL
½ tsp.	pepper	2 mL
½ tsp.	cinnamon	2 mL
16 oz.	jar grape leaves	454 mL
1	lemon, juice of	1
1	fresh lemon, cut into wedges	1
	water	

Combine lentils and water in a saucepan. Bring to a boil, cover and simmer for 30 minutes. Lentils can be a little firm. Drain.

Place bulgar in a large mixing bowl, add the hot water, set aside.

Heat oil in a skillet, add pine nuts, sauté until lightly browned. Add onions, sauté until transparent. Remove skillet from heat, add mint, lemon juice, seasonings, lentils and bulgar. Mix well, set aside.

Rinse grape leaves in warm water to remove the brine. Drain, remove stems. With the shiny side of the leaf down, place 1 tsp. (5 mL) of the filling in a line across the width of the leaf with the stem end closest to you. Fold the outside edges of the leaf ½" (1.3 cm) toward the center and roll with a little firmness into the shape of a finger. Place each roll with seam down, side by side in a large saucepan, stacking them until all are rolled. Add lemon juice and enough water to reach just below the last row rolled. Bring to a boil over medium heat, then lower heat. Cover and simmer for 1 hour, until leaves are tender.

Serve with fresh yogurt or as an appetizer with a squeeze of lemon juice over each serving.

VARIATIONS:
1. 2 large tomatoes, skinned and diced, or stewed tomatoes can be added to the filling.
2. Replace lentils and bulgar with the same amount of rice.

Garbanzo Beans with Raisins

Serves 4

A very tasty stew served over rice. Raisins add an interesting flavor. Turmeric gives an exotic yellow color to this dish.

1	large onion, sliced	1
2	garlic cloves, chopped	2
3 tbsp.	olive oil	45 mL
1 cup	diced zucchini	250 mL
1 cup	water or vegetable stock (page 72)	250 mL
½ cup	raisins	125 mL
1 tsp.	turmeric	5 mL
1 tsp.	cinnamon	5 mL
½ tsp.	ginger	2 mL
2 cups	garbanzo beans (chickpeas) cooked and drained	500 mL
2 cups	hot cooked rice	500 mL

Sauté onions and garlic in the oil in a 3-quart (3 L) saucepan over medium heat. Stir frequently, until tender, approximately 5 minutes.

Add remaining ingredients except garbanzo beans and rice. Heat to boiling, reduce heat. Cover and cook until the zucchini is tender, approximately 10 minutes. Stir in garbanzo beans.

Serve over rice.

See photograph on page 156.

Moujadara

Lentil Stew

Serves 3-4

This well-known peasant dish is Dan and Lou's favorite. The combination of lentils and rice has more nutritional value than each eaten separately.

1 cup	dried lentils, washed and drained	250 mL
6 cups	water or vegetable stock (page 72)	1.5 L
1 tsp.	salt	5 mL
¼ tsp.	pepper	1 mL
½ cup	rice, washed and drained	125 mL
1	medium onion, julienned	1
½ cup	vegetable oil	125 mL
	yogurt	
	pickles	
1	lemon, cut in ½	1

Wash lentils, drain and place in a saucepan. Add water. Cover and cook over medium heat for 1 hour, or until lentils are tender.

Add salt, pepper and rice to the lentils. Cook at a steady boil over low heat for 25 minutes, stirring occasionally.

Sauté onions in oil until golden brown. Add to the cooked lentil mixture; stir and remove from heat.

Serve hot or cold with fresh cold yogurt, pickles and a squeeze of lemon over each serving.

VARIATIONS:
1. 1 cup (250 mL) rice can be substituted for the ½ cup (125 mL) rice in recipe above. This will make the stew thicker, like a pilaf.
2. 1 cup (250 mL) coarse bulgar (crushed wheat) can be substituted for rice.
3. Heat ½ cup (125 mL) vegetable or olive oil in a small frying pan; add 1 medium onion, julienned. Cook until golden brown. Serve a heaping spoonful on top of each serving.

Khodra mah Adas

Vegetable Stew with Lentils

Serves 4-6

6 cups	water	1.5 L
1 cup	lentils, washed and drained	250 mL
1 cup	green beans	250 mL
3	large tomatoes, diced	3
1 cup	diced cabbage	250 mL
2	carrots, sliced	2
1	zucchini, cut into 1" (2.5 cm) slices	1
1 tsp.	salt	5 mL
½ tsp.	pepper	2 mL
1 tsp.	cinnamon	5 mL
½ tsp.	cumin	2 mL

Combine water and lentils in a large skillet or saucepan over high heat, then lower heat to medium. Skim off foam. Cover and cook until lentils are tender, approximately 1 hour.

Trim green beans, and cut into 1" (2.5 cm) pieces. Add to lentil mixture along with remaining vegetables. Cook until vegetables are tender, approximately 25 minutes. Add the remaining seasonings. Cook for 5 minutes more.

Serve with Rice Pilaf, page 85.

Vegetable Stew

Turmeric is used in this recipe. It gives the rice a yellow color. The use of this spice is widespread in the Middle East, Africa and India.

1 cup	chopped onions	250 mL
½ cup	chopped parsley	125 mL
3	garlic cloves, finely chopped	3
1 tsp.	cinnamon	5 mL
½ tsp.	ground turmeric	2 mL
½ tsp.	pepper	2 mL
½ tsp.	ground ginger	2 mL
2 tbsp.	butter	30 mL
5 cups	water or vegetable stock (page 72)	1.25 L
1 cup	sliced carrots	250 mL
½ cup	dried lentils	125 mL
1 cup	rice	250 mL
2	large ripe tomatoes, peeled and chopped	2
¾ tsp.	salt	3 mL
1½ cups	fresh or frozen green peas	375 mL
1½ cups	sliced fresh or frozen green beans	375 mL
¼ cup	coarsely chopped fresh mint	60 mL
	plain yogurt	

Place in a large skillet over medium heat, onions, parsley, garlic, cinnamon, turmeric, pepper, ginger and butter. Stir and cook until the onions are tender. Stir in the water, carrots and lentils. Bring to a boil, reduce heat, cover and cook for 25 minutes.

Add rice, tomatoes and salt. Heat to boiling then reduce heat. Cover and cook for 20 minutes. Stir in peas, beans and mint. Bring to a boil, reduce heat. Cover and cook for approximately 10 minutes. Beans will have a little crunch.

Add 1 tsp. (5 mL) of fresh yogurt on top of each serving.

Vegetarian Paella

This dish has become the most renowned of Spanish recipes. The name, "Paellera", refers to a large, heavy, shallow pan, round or oval, with side handles, in which this dish is prepared and served. Paella is a specialty from Valencia. This recipe is a vegetarian adaptation.

¼ cup	olive oil	60 mL
2½ cups	sliced mushrooms	625 mL
¼ cup	chopped green onions	60 mL
¼ cup	chopped red sweet peppers	60 mL
3	garlic cloves, sliced	3
½ tsp.	thyme	2 mL
1 tsp.	salt	5 mL
2 cups	short-grain rice	500 mL
4 cups	vegetable stock (page 72)	1 L
1	bay leaf, broken	1
½ tsp.	saffron	2 mL
¼ tsp.	pepper	1 mL
1½ cups	fresh or frozen green peas	375 mL
9 oz.	frozen artichoke hearts, may be partially thawed	280 g
	lemon wedges	

Heat oil in a large heavy saucepan or paellera. Add mushrooms, onions, peppers, garlic, thyme and salt. Cover and simmer for 5 minutes, stirring occasionally.

Add rice and next 4 ingredients, cover, bring to a boil. Reduce heat to low, cook for 25 minutes, or until rice is tender.

Add peas and artichokes, stir slightly and cover. Cook for 5 more minutes.

Serve on a large platter. Garnish with lemon wedges and Ali-oli (page 18).

VARIATIONS:
1. Garnish with slices of red or green peppers or olives.
2. Use the vegetables you prefer to substitute for the ones in this recipe.
3. Turmeric may be substituted for saffron.

See photograph on front cover.

Spain

Spain is primarily an agricultural country. It produces large crops of wheat, potatoes, barley, sugar cane, beets, citrus fruits, grapes and is world renowned for its aromatic and flavorful olive oil. Spices, especially saffron, turmeric, cumin, coriander, cinnamon, nutmeg and mace, appear in almost every dish.

Vegetables of all kinds are grown in abundance. There are culinary similarities between the regions, yet they each have their own specialties. For example, there is a strong Provençal influence in Catalonia in the use of aromatic herbs, garlic and mushrooms.

Although Mexico and Spain are oceans apart, their cuisines share a common interest. Many Mexican foods are wholly indigenous and existed long before the arrival of the Spaniards. Peppers of all kinds were brought to Spain from Mexico, and chickpeas were also transported to Mexico by the Spaniards. Spanish cuisine has a heritage from the long Moorish Arab occupations of the country many years ago. It was the Moors who brought rice into Spain. They also brought with them lentils, almonds, sugar cane and mint for flavoring.

The Tapas dishes of Spain have made their way into the Western world. These are delightful appetizers, quick to prepare and appropriate any time of day. Tapas bars are everywhere. They are filled with women returning from the market or men dropping in after work for a snack or a meal. Tapas are served in small dishes so one may sample different foods.

A light breakfast is served early. Lunch is usually served around 2-3 p.m., and consists of fruit and a light meal. Dinner is eaten between 9 p.m. to midnight and includes several courses. Paella (page 119) could very well be one of these dishes. This recipe is probably Spain's most famous contribution to international cuisine. Valencia is its place of origin, where rice is a main crop. Vegetables appear on the table with every meal.

Great wines are produced in this country. Spanish Sherry is world famous and is very much a part of Spanish cooking. It also precedes Tapas to prepare the palate properly for Spain's delicious cuisine.

Photograph Opposite

Top   — *Mezze Maniche alla Zingara (Gypsy Macaroni), page 142*
Center — *Spanish olives*
Bottom — *Churos (Fried Doughballs), page 153*

Koukia Yiahnt

Fava Bean Stew

½ cup	olive or vegetable oil	125 mL
1	large onion, chopped	1
4	celery stalks, chopped	4
2	medium carrots, chopped	2
3	garlic cloves, crushed	3
½ cup	tomato paste	125 mL
1½ cups	water or vegetable stock (page 72)	375 mL
2½ cups	fava beans, cooked	625 mL
½ tsp.	cinnamon	2 mL
	salt and pepper to taste	

Heat oil in a large saucepan. Add onions, celery and carrots. Sauté for 4-5 minutes. Add garlic, sauté for 2 minutes. Add tomato paste and water. Bring to a boil, simmer for 10 minutes. Add fava beans, cinnamon, salt and pepper.

Serve with Rice Pilaf (page 85) or Bulgar Pilaf (page 91).

See photograph on page 51.

Photograph Opposite — from top down

1. *Roasted Sweet Peppers, page 16*
2. *Escalibada (Grilled Vegetables), page 17*
3. *Green and Red Pepper Tapas, page 16*
4. *Fried Olives, page 21*
5. *Toasted Almonds, page 22*

Khodra Makhluta

Egyptian Stew

This combination of beans and vegetables is delicious served with Rice Pilaf (page 85).

4 tbsp.	olive oil	60 mL
4	garlic cloves, crushed	4
1 cup	chopped onions	250 mL
1¼ tsp.	salt	6 mL
1½ cups	thinly sliced potatoes	375 mL
1 tsp.	cinnamon	5 mL
1 tsp.	cumin	5 mL
½ tsp.	pepper	2 mL
¼ tsp.	crushed chili peppers	1 mL
3 tbsp.	lemon juice	45 mL
2	large carrots, thinly sliced	2
1	small cauliflower, divided into small florets	1
3	large tomatoes, cubed	3
2 tsp.	honey	10 mL
2 cups	cooked kidney beans	500 mL

Place olive oil, garlic, onions and salt in a large skillet. Sauté over medium heat until onions are transparent.

Add potatoes, spices and lemon juice. Cover and cook for 8 minutes, stirring occasionally. Add a little water if mixture sticks.

Add remaining ingredients except beans. Cover, cook gently over medium heat for approximately 30 minutes, stirring occasionally. Add the cooked beans, stir, cover and simmer for 10 minutes.

Serve with pita for scooping up portions of stew.

Gratin de Légumes

Vegetable Casserole

3	garlic cloves, minced	3
½ cup	olive oil	125 mL
4	large potatoes, peeled, sliced ⅛" (3 mm) thick	4
2	large zucchini, sliced ⅛" (3 mm) thick	2
12	Italian Roma (plum) tomatoes, sliced ½" (1.3 cm) thick	12
1 cup	shredded Gruyère cheese	250 mL
½ tsp.	oregano	2 mL
½ tsp.	basil	2 mL
1 tsp.	salt	5 mL
½ tsp.	pepper	2 mL
10	fresh basil leaves for garnish	10

Preheat oven to 425°F (220°C).

Combine garlic and oil in a small frying pan. Sauté for 5 minutes. Set aside.

In a 9 x 12" (23 x 30 cm) baking dish, layer ½ of the potatoes, zucchini, tomatoes, cheese, herbs and seasonings. Repeat layer of vegetables, cheese and herbs. Top with the oil and garlic mixture. Bake for 50 minutes, uncovered.

Coarsely chop the fresh basil, sprinkle on top of casserole before serving.

Serve hot.

See photograph on page 33.

Ratatouille

Vegetable Casserole

Serves 6-8

A very popular and wonderful dish from the south of France.

2	medium eggplants, approximately ½ lb. (250 g) each	2
2	medium zucchini	2
⅓ cup	olive oil	75 mL
2	garlic cloves, chopped	2
1	large onion, sliced in rings	1
1	large red pepper, seeded and cut into strips	1
1	large green pepper, seeded and cut into strips	1
3	large tomatoes, skinned and cubed	3
1½ tsp.	salt or to taste	7 mL
½ tsp.	pepper	2 mL
1	large bay leaf	1
½ tsp.	oregano	2 mL

Preheat oven to 400°F (200°C).

Cut eggplant and zucchini into ¾" (2 cm) cubes. Set aside.

Heat oil in a large skillet over medium heat. Add garlic and onion and cook until onion is transparent. Add the eggplant and zucchini. Sauté for 5 minutes, add peppers. Sauté for 4 more minutes. Add tomatoes and all seasonings and herbs. Stir gently to mix. Place in a 4-quart (4 L) casserole, cover and bake for 45 minutes.

Serve hot or cold as a main course.

See photograph on front cover.

Pisto Manchego

Vegetable Casserole

Serves 4

A tasty dish from La Mancha similar to the French ratatouille but firmer.

3 tbsp.	olive oil	45 mL
2	medium onions, cubed	2
2	medium zucchini, cubed	2
2	green peppers, cubed	2
4	large tomatoes, cubed	4
	salt	
	pepper	
1	egg, lightly beaten (optional)	1

Heat oil in a large saucepan and sauté the onions until they become transparent. Add the zucchini and peppers, cook slowly, partially covered, for 5 minutes.

Stir in the tomatoes and cook slowly for 10 more minutes. Season with salt and pepper to taste. Stir in beaten egg just before serving.

May be served on its own or as a side dish.

Bitinjan mah Hommous

Lebanon

Eggplant-Chickpea Stew

Serves 4

1	large onion, coarsely chopped	1
½ cup	vegetable oil	125 mL
½ cup	dried chickpeas, soaked overnight and drained	125 ml
3 cups	water	750 mL
1	large eggplant	1
1 tsp.	salt	5 mL
¼ tsp.	pepper	1 mL
¼ tsp.	cinnamon	1 mL
4	large, ripe tomatoes, diced	4

Place onions and oil in a saucepan. Cook until onions are golden brown. Add drained chickpeas and the water. Cook until chickpeas are tender, approximately 40 minutes.

Peel eggplant and cut into 1" (2.5 cm) cubes. Add to chickpea mixture. Add seasonings and diced tomatoes. Cover and cook for 20-25 minutes over medium heat, stirring occasionally until eggplant is tender.

May be served hot or cold.

Serve with Rice Pilaf (page 85).

Vegetable Stew Italiano

2	broccoli stalks, chopped	2
2	carrots, diced	2
2	celery stalks, chopped	2
1	eggplant, cubed	1
1 cup	sliced mushrooms	250 mL
1	large onion, chopped	1
1 cup	water or vegetable stock (page 72)	250 mL
	salt and pepper to taste	
⅓ cup	chopped flat-leaf Italian parsley	75 mL
3 tbsp.	chopped fresh basil	45 mL
½ tsp.	dried marjoram	2 mL
2 tsp.	olive oil	10 mL
2 tbsp.	grated Parmesan cheese	30 mL

Combine the vegetables and water in a large saucepan, add salt and pepper. Bring to a boil, cover and reduce heat. Simmer until vegetables are just tender, approximately 10-15 minutes. Add herbs and oil.

Serve hot or cold. Top each serving with Parmesan cheese.

Serve with any rice dish.

Turkish Vegetable Bake

Turkey

Serves 4-6

¼ cup	olive oil	60 mL
4	large garlic cloves, crushed	4
1 cup	chopped onions	250 mL
2 cups	sliced mushrooms	500 mL
3	medium eggplants, cut into 1" (2.5 cm) cubes	3
½ tsp.	dillweed	2 mL
½ tsp.	cumin	2 mL
1 tsp.	salt	5 mL
½ tsp.	lemon juice	2 mL
⅔ cup	raisins	150 mL
½ cup	bulgar	125 mL
1 tsp.	honey	5 mL
2 tbsp.	butter	30 mL
2 tbsp.	flour	30 mL
1¾ cups	hot milk	425 mL
2	eggs, hard-boiled, finely chopped	2

Preheat oven to 350°F (180°C).

Heat oil in a large heavy saucepan, add garlic and onions. Sauté over medium heat for 3-4 minutes. Stir in mushrooms, eggplant, seasoning and lemon juice. Cook, stirring frequently, for 5-8 minutes.

Add raisins, bulgar and honey. Stir well, cover. Simmer for 10-15 minutes, stirring frequently. When eggplant is just tender, remove from heat. Spread in an oiled 9 x 13" (22 x 33 cm) baking pan.

In a small saucepan, melt butter over low heat. Add flour and whisk for 2-3 minutes. Gradually add hot milk a little at a time, whisking constantly. Continue stirring with a wooden spoon for 5-8 minutes, until smooth and slightly thickened. Remove from heat, add the chopped eggs.

Pour this sauce over the eggplant mixture, spreading as evenly as possible.

Bake uncovered for 40-45 minutes.

Serve with a salad.

Ma'aloobi

Eggplant Casserole

Serves 4-6

Vegetarian style. A delicious one-of-a-kind recipe.

1 cup	pine nuts	250 mL
4 tbsp.	butter or vegetable oil	60 mL
1	medium onion, finely chopped	1
1½ tsp.	salt	7 mL
¼ tsp.	pepper	1 mL
2	large eggplants	2
3	large potatoes	3
4	large tomatoes	4
1	large onion	1
1 tsp.	salt	5 mL
¼ tsp.	pepper	1 mL
½ tsp.	cinnamon	2 mL
½ cup	tomato paste	125 mL
2½ cups	water	625 mL

Sauté pine nuts and butter in a skillet until nuts are golden brown. Add chopped onion, salt and pepper. Set aside.

Heat oven to 350°F (180°C). Peel eggplants and cut into ½" (1.3 cm) slices. Cut potatoes, tomatoes and onion into ¼" (1 cm) thick slices. Divide the vegetables evenly into 2 groups.

Layer the first group, alternating the 4 vegetables in a 9 x 12" (22 x 30 cm) baking pan. Spread with all the pine nut filling. Add the remaining vegetables, layering potatoes, eggplant, onions and lastly tomatoes. Sprinkle evenly with salt, pepper and cinnamon. Mix the tomato paste and water together in a small bowl and pour over all. Cover and bake for 1½ hours, or until all vegetables are tender.

Serve with Rice Pilaf (page 85).

Bitinjan Mah Fyllo

Lebanon

Eggplant Fyllo Layer

Serves 6-8

This recipe was created for The Cedars Restaurant and will not be found in any other cookbook. Absolutely delicious!

¼ cup	**vegetable oil**	60 mL
2	**medium eggplants, peeled and chopped**	2
2	**medium zucchini, chopped**	2
1	**large onion, chopped**	1
2 tsp.	**oregano**	10 mL
1 tsp.	**salt**	5 mL
½ tsp.	**pepper**	2 mL
½ lb.	**spinach with stems**	250 g
6	**eggs**	6
½ cup	**chopped parsley**	125 mL
6 tbsp.	**clarified butter, melted**	90 mL
16 oz.	**pkg. fyllo pastry dough**	500 g
1½ cups	**shredded mozzarella**	375 mL

NOTE:

Fyllo should be left out at room temperature at least 6 hours before using.

Set oven at 375°F (190°C).

Place first 7 ingredients in a large heavy saucepan. Sauté over medium heat until vegetables become limp, stirring occasionally, about 10 minutes. Remove from heat.

Wash spinach and drain. Set aside. In a mixing bowl, beat eggs slightly, add the parsley. Set aside.

Butter an 8 x 14" (20 x 35 cm) baking pan with 2 tbsp. (30 mL) of the clarified butter. Place ½ of the fyllo sheets in the pan, folding them to fit the bottom of the pan, right up to the edges. Cover remainder of fyllo with damp cloth. Add the eggplant mixture, spreading evenly. Add the spinach leaves, covering all the eggplant. Spoon the egg mixture over the spinach. Sprinkle evenly with the cheese. Place sheets of fyllo over the top. Fold in the edges to fit to the rim of the pan. Spread the remaining 4 tbsp. (60 mL) of butter over the top sheet. Cut into rectangles or squares. Bake for 45 minutes, or until golden brown.

Delicious with fresh yogurt or salad.

See photograph on page 87.

Moussaka

A very popular dish and very nutritious. A lengthy process, but worth it.

SAUCE FOR TOPPING

½ cup	butter	125 mL
6 tbsp.	flour	90 mL
4 cups	hot milk	1 L
4	eggs, slightly beaten	4
1 cup	grated kefalotiri or Parmesan cheese	250 mL
½ tsp.	salt	2 mL
¼ tsp.	white pepper	1 mL
¼ tsp.	nutmeg	1 mL
2	medium eggplants	2
¼ cup	salt	60 mL
3	medium zucchini, cut into ¼" (1 cm) slices	3
3	large potatoes, peeled and cut into ⅛" (3 mm) slices	3
½ cup	olive oil	125 mL
1	large onion, finely chopped	1
3	garlic cloves, minced	3
2 cups	sliced mushrooms	500 mL
½ cup	bulgar	125 mL
2½ cups	crushed tomatoes	625 mL
½ cup	red wine	125 mL
2½ cups	water	625 mL
½ cup	finely chopped parsley	125 mL
2 tbsp.	finely chopped oregano or 1 tbsp. (15 mL) dry	30 mL
1½ tsp.	salt	7 mL
½ tsp.	pepper	2 mL
½ tsp.	cinnamon	2 mL
¾ cup	bread crumbs	175 mL
1 cup	grated kefalotiri or Parmesan cheese	250 mL

To prepare the sauce, melt the butter in a large heavy saucepan over medium heat. Add the flour and stir to blend. Gradually add the milk, then the eggs, stirring constantly over medium heat. Lower heat and continue stirring for approximately 10 minutes, until sauce is smooth and thickened. Add the grated cheese, stir, cook on low heat for 2-3 minutes more, stirring constantly. Remove from heat. Stir in the salt, pepper and nutmeg. Set aside.

Moussaka

Continued

Cut the eggplants lengthwise into ¼" (1 cm) slices, sprinkle with the ¼ cup (60 mL) salt. Place in a colander to drain for 30 minutes.

Place the zucchini and potatoes in cold water and add a little salt to prevent the potatoes from browning.

Heat oil in a large skillet. Add onions and garlic, sauté over medium heat until onions are transparent. Add the mushrooms and bulgar, sauté for 2-3 minutes. Add the next 8 ingredients. Stir and cook for 1 minute to mix well. Remove from heat.

Heat oven to 400°F (200°C).

Butter a 10 x 15" (25 x 38 cm) baking pan. Sprinkle ½ of the bread crumbs and ½ cup (125 mL) of the cheese in the pan.

Rinse the eggplant and wipe dry with paper towels. Arrange ½ of the eggplant in the bottom of the pan. Then layer ½ of the zucchini and ½ of the potatoes. Add all of the vegetable and bulgar mixture, spreading evenly to the sides. Sprinkle the remaining bread crumbs evenly. Continue to layer, beginning with potatoes and ending with eggplant. Pour the sauce evenly over the top. Sprinkle with the remaining ½ cup (125 mL) of cheese.

Bake for 1 hour, or until golden brown.

After removing Moussaka from the oven, let it set for 10 minutes before cutting.

Berenjenas a la Mudejar

Stuffed Baked Eggplant

This recipe was brought into Spain by Muslim Arabs called the Mudejar people.

4	large eggplants	4
1½ tsp.	salt	7 mL
¼ cup	olive oil	60 mL
2	garlic cloves, finely chopped	2
3	large tomatoes, skinned and chopped	3
1	large onion, finely chopped	1
2 tbsp.	toasted slivered almonds	30 mL
	salt and pepper to taste	
½ cup	bread crumbs	125 mL
3 tbsp.	chopped parsley	45 mL
4 tbsp.	grated strong cheese	60 mL

Cut the eggplant in half lengthwise. Scoop out the pulp and reserve, leaving a ¾" (2 cm) shell. Sprinkle inside of shell with salt and let stand for 30 minutes. Chop the reserved pulp, set aside.

Heat oil in a skillet and sauté the garlic, tomatoes, onions, almonds and chopped eggplant pulp for 5-10 minutes, stirring frequently, until a thick paste is obtained. Season with salt and pepper to taste.

Set oven at 350°F (180°C).

Pat the eggplant shells with paper towels and fill them with the sautéed mixture. Arrange in a greased baking dish. Sprinkle shells with bread crumbs, parsley and cheese. Bake for 30 minutes.

Serve hot or cold. This is an excellent main dish, served with a salad.

Parmigiana di Melanzane

Italy

Eggplant with Parmesan Cheese

Serves 6

A wonderful main-course dish, with the eggplant broiled rather than sautéed. Eggplant is treasured in the Mediterranean and is frequently used in Italian cooking. Mushrooms or strips of green pepper can be added to the sauce.

2	medium eggplants, approximately 1½ lbs. (750 g), peeled	2
	salt	
¼ cup	olive oil	60 mL
4	shallots, peeled and chopped	4
4	large plum tomatoes, chopped	4
3 tbsp.	chopped Italian parsley	45 mL
3 tbsp.	chopped fresh basil	45 mL
¼ cup	grated fresh Parmesan cheese	60 mL
¼ cup	shredded mozzarella cheese	60 mL

Preheat broiler.

Cut eggplants into thin slices, place in a colander, sprinkle lightly with salt, set aside for 10 minutes.

Rinse eggplant and pat dry. Brush with some of the olive oil and place on a baking sheet in a single layer. Broil for 5 minutes, or until lightly browned on 1 side only. Set aside.

Heat oven to 350°F (180°C).

Heat remaining oil in a small frying pan, add the shallots and sauté over medium heat for 1 minute. Add the tomatoes and herbs. Cook for 10 minutes stirring occasionally.

Spread the sauce over the bottom of a 9 x 13" (23 x 33 cm) baking dish. Arrange eggplant over the sauce. Sprinkle with Parmesan cheese, then mozzarella cheese. Bake for 15-20 minutes.

Serve from the baking dish with Insalata Caprese (page 39) or Insalata Verde (page 36).

Pizza

Usually Italian pizza dough is mixed and kneaded on a flat surface. This recipe is mixed in a bowl then turned onto a flat surface for kneading. The Focaccia recipe (page 93) can also be used.

1½ tsp.	**dry yeast**	7 mL
1 cup	**lukewarm water**	250 mL
4 cups	**flour (approximately)**	1 L
1 tsp.	**salt**	5 mL
	olive oil	

Add yeast to the water, stir slightly and let stand until yeast softens, about 5 minutes.

Place 3 cups (750 mL) of flour in a large mixing bowl. Make a well in the center, add salt and 2 tbsp. (30 mL) of oil. Begin mixing the yeast mixture into the flour a little at a time, until flour has been absorbed. Turn dough onto a floured flat surface. Continue adding flour a little at a time, kneading vigorously, until the dough is smooth and elastic. Dough should be somewhat soft.

Grease the same bowl the dough was made in; add dough and turn it over to grease the top so it is greased all over. Cover with a tea towel or cloth. Let rise in a warm place until double in bulk, approximately 1½-2 hours.

TOPPING:

This topping is very basic; make your own additions or use suggestions below.

2 cups	**ripe tomatoes, peeled and chopped or canned Italian plum tomatoes**	500 mL
2 tsp.	**oregano**	10 mL
¼ tsp.	**pepper**	1 mL
1 cup	**diced or shredded mozzarella cheese**	250 mL
⅓ cup	**grated Parmesan cheese**	75 mL

Pizza
Continued

Preheat oven to 475°F (240°C).

Roll out dough and place in a greased 12 x 14" (30 x 35 cm) baking pan or use 2 small pizza pans.

Press the dough out to the edges of pan using fingers to stretch the dough.

Spread the tomatoes over the dough. Sprinkle with oregano, pepper and mozzarella; top with Parmesan cheese.

Bake the large pizza for approximately 25 minutes, and the smaller ones for 15-20 minutes in the hottest part of the oven, near the bottom. Pizza should be lightly browned.

Cut into squares or wedges and serve immediately.

SUGGESTIONS FOR TOPPINGS:
Sliced mushrooms, chopped red or green peppers, artichokes, pineapple, olives, thinly sliced zucchini, shrimp, anchovies, feta cheese, chopped fresh basil, etc.

Fettuccine al Pesto

Fettuccine with Pesto

This is a classic sauce for fettuccine. Pesto means to pound or pulverize. Traditionally done with mortar and pestle, today pesto is whipped up in a blender or food processor. Sometimes marjoram and mint are blended into the pesto.

2	garlic cloves	2
1 tbsp.	pine nuts	15 mL
2½ cups	basil leaves	625 mL
¼ tsp.	salt	1 mL
¼ tsp.	pepper	1 mL
1 cup	grated Romano cheese	250 mL
¼ tsp.	cayenne pepper	1 mL
1 cup	olive oil	250 mL
1 lb.	fettuccine noodles	500 g
	pinch of bicarbonate of soda	
½ cup	cold water	125 mL
¼ cup	boiling vegetable stock (page 72) or water	60 mL

Combine, in a blender or food processor, the first 7 ingredients and ½ of the oil. Blend on low speed until mixture forms a paste. Continue blending on low speed, gradually adding the remainder of the oil. Set aside.

Cook noodles following package directions. Before removing from stove, add the bicarbonate of soda and cold water to keep noodles firm and well separated. Drain the noodles. Just before serving, add the boiling vegetable stock to the pesto, stir well.

Top the hot fettuccini with pesto sauce or mix together.

NOTE:
Any pasta can be substituted for the fettuccine.

See photograph on page 70.

Pasta con Pesto

Italy

Pasta with Pesto Sauce

Serves 4

Another variation for pesto sauce and noodles. This pasta dish has a sauce similar to the French pistou.

1½ cups	chopped basil leaves	375 mL
⅓ cup	grated Parmesan cheese	75 mL
⅓ cup	olive oil	75 mL
2 tbsp.	pine nuts or walnuts	30 mL
½ tsp.	salt	2 mL
¼ tsp.	pepper	1 mL
2	garlic cloves	2
10 oz.	spaghetti or noodles	285 g
2 tbsp.	butter	30 mL

Combine all ingredients except spaghetti and butter in a blender or food processor. Blend until mixture is finely chopped but not puréed.

Cook spaghetti according to package directions and drain.

Toss spaghetti with pesto sauce and the butter. Serve with additional Parmesan cheese if desired.

Pasta Florentine

Noodles with Spinach

Serves 6-8

2 lbs.	noodles, any kind, cooked according to pkg. directions	1 kg
½ cup	olive oil	125 mL
2	garlic cloves, minced	2
½ cup	grated fresh Swiss or Gruyère cheese	125 mL
	pepper to taste	
6 cups	cooked spinach, chopped	1.5 L
2 tsp.	dried tarragon	10 mL
3 tbsp.	lemon juice	45 mL
½ cup	butter	125 mL
	salt	
	buttered, toasted bread crumbs	
	freshly grated Parmesan cheese	

Preheat broiler.

Drain noodles and mix them with the oil, garlic, cheese and pepper to taste. Set aside.

Drain spinach and add the tarragon, lemon juice, butter and salt to taste.

Make a bed of the hot spinach on the bottom of a lightly greased 9 x 13" (23 x 33 cm) baking dish. Place noodles on top and sprinkle liberally with the bread crumbs and Parmesan cheese. Put under the broiler for 5 minutes.

Serve at once with Italian bread or salad.

Spaghetti con le Melanzane

Italy

Spaghetti with Eggplant

Serves 6

2	medium eggplants	2
	salt	
	pepper	
	olive oil	
3	garlic cloves, crushed	3
4	large ripe tomatoes	4
¼ cup	finely chopped basil	60 mL
1 lb.	spaghetti	500 g
¼ cup	grated Parmesan cheese	60 mL

Peel the eggplant and cut into thin slices. Sprinkle with 3 tbsp. (45 mL) of salt and leave to drain in a colander for 1 hour. Wipe the slices dry with paper towel or cloth. Fry slices in hot oil a few at a time, brown on both sides. Add a little more oil to coat the pan each time. Drain on paper towels.

Pour about ¼ cup (60 mL) oil into a small frying pan, sauté the garlic cloves until brown and discard them. Peel and chop the tomatoes, discarding the seeds. Stir the tomatoes into the garlic oil and cook for 20 minutes on medium heat. Add salt and pepper to taste and the basil.

Bring a large pan of salted water to a boil. Add the spaghetti and cook until tender but still firm. Drain and immediately top with fried eggplant, tomato sauce and cheese. Serve at once with additional cheese.

See photograph on page 69.

Mezze Maniche alla Zingara

Gypsy Macaroni

Simple to prepare and very flavorful and colorful.

1 lb.	macaroni or rigatoni	500 g
6	large tomatoes, peeled, seeded and chopped	6
¼ cup	olive oil	60 mL
3	garlic cloves	3
1	red pepper, seeded and chopped	1
1	green pepper, seeded and chopped	1
¼ cup	chopped basil	60 mL
12	pitted black olives, chopped	12
¼ tsp.	oregano	1 mL
½ tsp.	salt	2 mL
¼ tsp.	pepper	1 mL

Cook the macaroni according to package directions.

While macaroni is cooking, prepare the sauce. Drain the chopped tomatoes. Heat the oil in a saucepan and sauté the garlic and peppers. Add the tomatoes, basil, olives, oregano, salt and pepper. Cook the sauce over low heat until it thickens, approximately 15-20 minutes.

When the pasta is cooked, drain and top with the sauce. Serve with garlic bread and Parmesan cheese.

See photograph on page 121.

Sweet Treats

Sliced Oranges with Dates

Serves 4-6

Moroccans love oranges and dates. Together they create an exciting dessert.

4	**large oranges, peeled and sliced**	4
½ **cup**	**pitted dates, quartered**	125 mL
2 **tbsp.**	**toasted slivered almonds**	30 mL
1 **tsp.**	**rose water**	5 mL
	fresh mint leaves (optional)	

Arrange orange slices on a serving platter. Sprinkle with dates and toasted almonds. Drizzle with the rosewater. Cover and refrigerate at least 3 hours. Garnish with mint leaves.

NOTE:
A distillation of rose petals, rosewater can be purchased in Middle Eastern grocery stores. It has an intense flavor and fragrance of roses. It has been used for hundreds of years in the Middle East.

See photograph on page 155.

Salatat Fwaki

Fresh Fruit Salad

3	oranges, peeled and cut into sections	3
3	tangerines, peeled and cut into sections	3
3	apples, cored and sliced	3
	green grapes	
	red grapes	
3	peaches, pitted and sliced	3
	any other fresh fruit in season	
	fresh mint sprigs	
	Yogurt Sauce (recipe below)	

Arrange fruit on a large platter. Garnish with mint.

YOGURT SAUCE

¼ cup	orange juice	60 mL
1 cup	yogurt	250 mL
½ tsp.	orange-flower water (optional)	2 mL
2 tbsp.	chopped pistachio nuts	30 mL

Combine the orange juice, yogurt and orange-flower water in a mixing bowl. Mix well. Place in a small serving bowl and sprinkle with pistachio nuts. Place bowl in center of fruit platter for dipping.

NOTE:

Orange-flower water is the essence of the orange tree blossom. It can be purchased in Middle Eastern grocery stores.

Apple Dessert

Serves 3

A delicious fruit dessert. Rose water can be purchased in specialty food stores or pharmacies. A similar recipe was used during Biblical times.

3	medium apples, pared and cut up	3
3 tbsp.	sugar	45 mL
1 tbsp.	lemon juice	15 mL
1 tbsp.	rose water (optional)	15 mL

Place all ingredients in blender or food processor. Blend for 20-30 seconds. Leave coarsely chopped. Serve chilled.

VARIATION:
1. This can be topped with any berries in season.

Biscuit Tortoni

Italy

Serves 10-12

A classic frozen Italian dessert.

1½ cups	whipping cream, chilled	375 mL
⅓ cup	sugar	75 mL
1 cup	vanilla wafer crumbs	250 mL
½ cup	lightly toasted flaked blanched almonds	125 mL
¼ cup	drained and chopped maraschino cherries	60 mL
2 tbsp.	rum or dry sherry	30 mL
1 tsp.	vanilla	5 mL

Beat cream and sugar in a chilled bowl until stiff. Fold in ¾ cup (175 mL) of vanilla wafer crumbs and remaining ingredients. Divide among 10-12 small dessert dishes. Sprinkle with remaining crumbs. Freeze until firm, approximately 4 hours.

Flan al Caramelo

Spanish Caramel Custard

Serves 4-5

This baked custard is one of the most popular Spanish desserts.

8 tbsp.	sugar	125 mL
1 tsp.	water	5 mL
½ tsp.	coriander	2 mL
2 cups	milk	500 mL
½ tsp.	vanilla	2 mL
3	eggs	3

Heat oven to 350°F (180°C).

Place 6 tbsp. (90 mL) of sugar and the water in a heavy frying pan. Bring to a boil over low heat, stirring constantly to dissolve sugar. Boil over high heat, do not stir. Watch for syrup to change to a golden color. Remove from heat. Evenly distribute the caramel into 4 or 5 custard cups to coat part way up. Cool until firm.

Combine the coriander and milk in a heavy saucepan. heat to almost boiling, add the remaining sugar and vanilla. Cook, stirring frequently, for 2-3 minutes. Set aside to cool.

Beat eggs until frothy. Stir in the milk. Strain the custard and pour into prepared custard cups.

Place the cups into a small roasting pan containing 1" (2.5 cm) of hot water. Cover cups with a sheet of waxed paper. Bake for 45 minutes, or until a knife comes out clean when inserted into the center of the custard. If water boils over, lower oven temperature slightly.

Serve chilled.

Leche Frita

Fried Milk

A creamy custard coated with a golden crust.

½ cup	sugar	125 mL
½ cup	cornstarch	125 mL
¼ tsp.	nutmeg	1 mL
3 cups	milk	750 mL
1 tbsp.	butter	15 mL
½ tsp.	grated lemon rind	2 mL
2	eggs, well-beaten	2
1 cup	bread crumbs	250 mL
	vegetable oil for frying	
	icing sugar (optional)	

Mix sugar, cornstarch and nutmeg in a 3-quart (3 L) saucepan. Gradually stir in milk. Heat to boiling over medium heat, stirring constantly. Boil and stir for 1 minute. Remove from heat. Stir in butter and lemon rind. Spread evenly in an ungreased 8" (20 cm) square pan. Refrigerate for 3 hours, or until firm.

Heat oil, 1½" (4 cm) deep, to 360°F (185°C) in a large frying pan.

Cut custard into 2" (5 cm) squares with a wet knife. Dip custard into the beaten eggs. Coat with the bread crumbs. Fry 3-4 squares at a time, on both sides, until golden brown, about 1-2 minutes. Drain and sprinkle with icing sugar if desired.

Serve hot.

Rizogalo

Rice Pudding

Serves 6-8

Every country in the Mediterranean has its own version of this recipe.

5 cups	milk	1.25 L
1 tsp.	grated lemon rind	5 mL
½ cup	rice, rinsed and drained	125 mL
½ cup	sugar	125 mL
2	eggs, beaten	2
1 tsp.	vanilla	5 mL
	cinnamon	

Combine 4 cups (1 L) of the milk, lemon rind and rice in a large heavy saucepan. Cook over medium heat, stirring often to prevent mixture from sticking. Bring to a boil. Cook for 20 minutes, stirring frequently. Place the sugar in a small mixing bowl, add the eggs, vanilla and remaining milk. Blend together. Slowly stir into the rice mixture. Simmer for 15 minutes, stirring occasionally, until mixture thickens. The rice will rise to the top when done. Do not overcook. Pour into serving bowls.

Cool, sprinkle each serving with cinnamon. Refrigerate.

Baklawa

Baklava

The Queen of Lebanese pastries. Famous throughout the world.

	Syrup recipe (page 151)	
1 lb.	**fyllo dough**	**500 g**
2 cups	**finely chopped walnuts, pistachios or almonds**	**500 mL**
½ cup	**sugar (optional)**	**125 mL**
1½ cups	**clarified butter**	**375 mL**

Prepare syrup recipe. Let cool before pouring over baklava.

If fyllo is frozen, defrost at room temperature for 6 hours.

When working with fyllo dough, always keep sheets that are not being used covered with a damp cloth.

Combine nuts and sugar, mixing well. Set aside.

Butter the bottom of a 10 x 14" (25 x 35 cm) baking pan.

Divide the package of fyllo dough into 2 sections, ½ for the bottom layer and the other ½ for the top.

To clarify butter, melt the butter over low to medium heat. Bring to a boil. Remove from heat, skim off foam. Use only the clear butter. Do not use any with the milk residue at the bottom.

Lay 2 sheets of fyllo over the bottom of the pan. Brush with clarified butter, then take 2 more sheets and lay them over the 2 in the pan. Repeat this procedure until ½ of the fyllo dough is used. Spoon the nuts evenly over the last layer.

With the remaining fyllo, continue to butter 2 sheets of fyllo, as above, and place them over the nut layer, repeating the same procedure until all sheets are used. Drizzle remaining butter over all. Cut into 1½" (4 cm) rectangular or diamond-shaped pieces.

Bake at 300°F (150°C) for 1 hour, or until golden brown. Remove from oven and pour cold syrup over the baklava, saturating well.

Baklawa

Continued

VARIATION:
For a different-shaped baklava, take 2 fyllo sheets and brush lightly with melted butter. Place 3-4 tbsp. (45-60 mL) of the filling along the wide edge of the fyllo. Roll as a jelly roll. Brush butter along the top. Cut diagonally into 2" (5 cm) lengths. Place close together on buttered 10 x 14" (25 x 35 cm) pan. Continue until fyllo and nut filling is used up. Bake at 300°F (150°C) for 45 minutes, or until golden brown. Remove from oven. Spoon cold syrup over each piece, saturating well.

See photograph on page 87.

Atter

Lebanon

Syrup for Baklava

2 cups	sugar or honey	500 mL
1 cup	water	250 mL
1 tbsp.	lemon juice	30 mL
1	geranium leaf or ½ tsp. (2 mL) rose water (optional)	1

If honey is substituted for sugar use only ½ cup (125 mL) water in the recipe and follow these directions.

Combine sugar and water. Stir until sugar is dissolved. Boil over medium heat for 5 minutes.

Add lemon juice and geranium leaf or rose water if desired. Boil for 5 more minutes. Remove from heat and cool.

Tarte Tatin

France

Apple Pie

Serves 6

This is an open-faced pie.

1	**single pastry shell (recipe below)**	1
6	**large tart apples**	6
¼ cup	**sugar**	60 mL
4 tbsp.	**melted butter**	60 mL

Preheat oven to 450°F (230°C).

Prepare pastry shell.

Peel and core apples. Cut into thin crescents. Arrange and layer apples on pastry shell in a pinwheel pattern. Sprinkle with sugar and drizzle butter on top.

Bake for 45 minutes.

VARIATION:
Fresh peaches may be used instead of apples and for a very delicately flavored pie try fresh pears.

See photograph on page 34.

Single Pastry Shell

France

Makes 1

1½ cups	**sifted flour**	375 mL
½ tsp.	**salt**	2 mL
⅓ cup	**vegetable oil**	75 mL
5 tbsp.	**cold water or as needed**	75 mL

Place flour and salt in mixing bowl. Add oil, mix until mixture resembles oatmeal.

Add water a little at a time, using enough to hold the dough together. Shape dough into a ball. Do not knead.

Lightly flour board and roll out dough with rolling pin to 1" (2.5 cm) larger than the 9" (23 cm) pie plate. Transfer the rolled dough onto the pie plate. Fold the edges over the rim of the pie plate. Flute or pinch with fingers to make a decorative border. Keep chilled until ready to use or freeze.

To make 2 shells, double recipe.

Churos

Fried Doughballs

Serves 5-6

Serve these delicious fritters for breakfast or as tapas.

1 cup	water	250 mL
½ cup	butter	125 mL
⅛ tsp.	salt	0.5 mL
1¼ cups	sifted all-purpose flour	300 mL
4	eggs	4
2 tsp.	grated orange rind	10 mL
	vegetable oil for frying	
	sifted icing sugar	

Combine water, butter and salt in a saucepan over medium heat. When butter is melted and water starts to boil, remove from heat. Add flour, stir hard with a wooden spoon until paste is smooth and dough becomes a little darker.

Return to heat. Stir until paste comes away from the sides of the pan.

Remove from heat, place in a small mixing bowl. Beat in eggs, 1 at a time, beating well after each addition. Scrape sides and beaters occasionally. Stir in orange rind .

Heat oil, 3-4" (7-10 cm) deep, to 375°F (190°C). Drop dough by the teaspoonful (5 mL) into hot oil, frying a few at a time.

Fritters will puff as they cook. Remove with slotted spoon when golden brown, drain on paper towels.

Sprinkle with icing sugar. Serve hot.

NOTE:
To keep warm, place in oven.

See photograph on page 121.

Egypt

This mysterious country is known as the land of the Pharaohs and it is renown for the spectacular pyramids. It was once the home of Cleopatra.

Geographically Egypt is a desert. The Nile river runs from south to north, and along its length is a fertile valley and delta. Carefully controlled irrigation from the Nile river and the hot climate affords Egypt a long growing season. Despite the virtual absence of rain, they are able to harvest two to three times a year. There is, however, a winter rainfall on the Mediterranean coast.

Fruits and vegetables of all kinds are grown in Egypt. They also cultivate sugar cane and cereal grains, but cotton is by far the main crop. The imaginative use of bulgar, artichokes, milookhiyya leaves, chickpeas, lentils, fava beans, garlic, coriander and cumin creates delicious and flavorful meals fit for a king.

As in many hot countries, a breakfast of eggs, cheese, olives and yogurt is usually served early. Lunch is served around 2:00-3:00 p.m. and is the largest meal of the day. At this time some of the many dishes could include Roasted (page 83) or Bulgar-Stuffed Peppers (page 110) and Artichoke and Green Bean Casserole (page 97) with vegetables or salads. Dinner is served around 8:00 p.m. This meal is lighter and may consist of Egyptian Milookhiyya Soup (page 66), salads and pita bread, fruit and vegetables.

Alcohol is not served with meals in this country due to the predominant Muslim religion. Arabic coffee, in demitasse cups, is served regularly throughout the day.

Photograph Opposite

Top — *Michoteta (Vegetable Feta Cheese Salad — Egypt), page 37*
Center — *Sliced Oranges with Dates (Morocco), page 144*
Bottom — *Couscous Vegetarian Style (Morocco), page 111*

Morocco

The coastal regions of Morocco have the most rainfall. In parts of the Rif, where wheat and cereal grains are grown without irrigation, some 40" of rain fall each year. There are extensive plains on the Atlantic coast where olives, citrus fruits and grapes are grown.

During the 19th century the French brought to Morocco their exquisite knowledge of food preparation. Bread is a good example of French influence. A breakfast of fruit, vegetables and eggs is served early. Lunch is eaten in the early afternoon and is the largest meal of the day. It may consist of Couscous (page 111), Garbanzo Beans with Raisins (page 115), bread, vegetables and a large platter of fresh fruit. A late dinner is served around 8:00 p.m. It may be Vegetarian El-Harirah Soup (page 63) with bread and some fruit.

Moroccan dishes are typified by the skillful use of turmeric, saffron, coriander and ginger. These spices produce intriguing dishes which will always be fondly remembered. Mint tea is served with all meals. This refreshing tea is made with fresh mint leaves and served in a glass.

Turkey

This country is predominantly agricultural with very fertile coastal strips. Almost half of its area consists of pasture used for the raising of cattle, sheep, goats and water buffalo. The land produces wheat, barley, oats, rye, maize, tobacco and cotton. Grapes, raisins, olives, figs, apples, hazelnuts and walnuts are grown extensively. Citrus fruits are grown around the Mersin area.

There is much Armenian influence in Turkish cuisine, as the north-east part of Asiatic Turkey forms part of Armenia.

Breakfast is served early and may consist of yogurt and fruit. Lunch is served in the late afternoon and is the largest meal of the day. A typical lunch could be Grape Leaves Stuffed with Lentils and Bulgar (page 114), Turkish Fava Bean Salad (page 26) and Yogurt Dessert (page 160). Dinner could be Turkish Cucumber Salad (page 29), fruit, vegetables and bread. Turkish coffee is served often. This coffee is very strong and is served in demitasse cups.

Photograph Opposite

Left — *Fleifleh Mishwi (Egypt), page 83*
Right — *Turkish Eggplant Salad (Turkey), page 25*
Bottom — *Garbanzo Beans with Raisins (Morocco), page 115*

Cicerchiata

Honey Cake

2¼ cups	flour	550 mL
½ cup	sugar	125 mL
5 tbsp.	olive oil	75 mL
2	eggs, slightly beaten	2
	oil for frying	
7 oz.	honey	200 g
1 tbsp.	slivered blanched almonds	15 mL
	cinnamon	
	icing sugar	

Sift flour into a mixing bowl, make a well in the center, add sugar, oil and eggs. Work the batter to form a firm dough. Add a bit more flour if necessary, knead until smooth and pliable.

Break off a piece of the dough and roll into a long thin rope, about 12" (30 cm) long. Cut into tiny balls, a little larger than a pea. Repeat with remaining dough.

In a large frying pan, heat oil on medium heat for deep frying. Drop the dough peas into the oil a few at a time. Fry until golden, remove with a slotted spoon and place on paper towels.

Melt the honey in a saucepan large enough to hold all of the fried dough balls. Cook until honey starts to change color. Add the fried dough balls, stir carefully with a wooden spoon to mix well.

Turn onto a plate brushed with water. When the mixture has cooled enough to touch, shape into a ring. Shape like a large doughnut. Sprinkle with the slivered almonds, cinnamon and sifted icing sugar.

Panettone

Italian Coffee Cake

Makes 2 loaves

A festive sweet bread from Milan with raisins, lemon peel and citron. This is the Italian Christmas cake.

2 tbsp.	active dry yeast (2 envelopes)	30 mL
1 cup	warm water	250 mL
½ cup	sugar	125 mL
½ cup	butter, softened	125 mL
4	eggs	4
1 tsp.	salt	5 mL
2 tsp.	grated lemon peel	10 mL
1½ tsp.	vanilla	7 mL
5-5½ cups	flour	1.25-1.35 L
½ cup	golden raisins	125 mL
½ cup	chopped citron	125 mL
3 tbsp.	pine nuts or walnuts (optional)	45 mL
	butter, softened	

Dissolve yeast in 1 cup (250 mL) of warm water in a large bowl. Stir in the sugar, ½ cup (125 mL) butter, eggs, salt, lemon peel, vanilla and 2½ cups (625 mL) of flour. Beat until smooth. Stir in the raisins, citron, nuts and enough of the remaining flour to make the dough easy to handle.

Turn dough onto a lightly floured surface. Knead for about 5 minutes until smooth and elastic. Place in greased bowl. Turn dough greased side up. Cover, let rise in a warm place until doubled, approximately 1½-2 hours. Punch down dough and divide in half. Shape each into a round loaf 7" (18 cm) in diameter.

Place loaves into 2 ungreased 8" (20 cm) round layer pans. Cut a cross ½" (1.3 cm) deep on top of each loaf. Generously grease 1 side of a strip of heavy brown paper, about 4½ x 25" (12 x 43 cm). Fit around the inside of the pan forming a circle. Fasten with paper clips. Repeat for the second pan. Cover, let rise until doubled, approximately 1 hour.

Heat oven to 350°F (180°C). Bake loaves until golden brown, about 35-40 minutes. Remove paper. Brush tops with butter. Cool on rack.

Yogurt Dessert

A Turkish dessert to remember!

1 cup	yogurt	250 mL
1½ cups	icing sugar	375 mL
3	eggs	3
¼ cup	melted butter	60 mL
2 cups	sifted flour	500 mL
1 tbsp.	grated orange or lemon rind	15 mL
1 tsp.	baking powder	5 mL
2½ cups	granulated sugar	625 mL
3 cups	water	750 mL
1 tbsp.	lemon juice	15 mL
3 tbsp.	ground pistachio nuts	45 mL
	whipping cream	
2 cups	strawberries	500 mL

Heat oven to 350°F (180°C).

Grease a 9" (23 cm) square baking pan.

Place yogurt in a mixing bowl. Beat with mixer, gradually beating in the icing sugar, eggs, butter, flour and rind. Batter should be smooth. Add baking powder, beating lightly. Do not overbeat.

Pour batter into the prepared pan and bake for 40-45 minutes.

While cake is baking, 15 minutes before it's done, make the syrup.

Combine the sugar, water and lemon juice in a saucepan. Bring to a boil, stirring until sugar is dissolved. Simmer for 10 minutes. Remove from heat and keep hot.

Cut the cake into serving pieces. Pour hot syrup over all, a little at a time. Cool.

To serve, sprinkle cake with pistachio nuts. Arrange on a serving dish and serve with whipped cream and strawberries.

Sfoof

Turmeric Cake

Turmeric gives this cake a beautiful golden color and delicious flavor.

2½ cups	semolina or Cream of Wheat	625 mL
2 tbsp.	turmeric	30 mL
4 tbsp.	powdered milk	60 mL
3 tsp.	baking powder	15 mL
2 cups	sugar	500 mL
1½ cups	water	375 mL
1 cup	butter, melted	250 mL
¼ cup	tahini (sesame seed paste)	60 mL

Set oven at 375°F (190°C).

Place semolina in mixing bowl, add turmeric, milk and baking powder. Dissolve the sugar in the water. Add this and the butter to the flour mixture. Beat well for 5 minutes.

Grease the bottom and sides of an 8" (20 cm) square baking pan with tahini.

Pour the batter gently into the pan and bake for 20-25 minutes.

Cool before cutting with a sharp knife. This cake has a dry texture. Serve for afternoon tea.

Ravani

Cream of Wheat Cake

Serves 10-12

1 cup	unsalted butter, room temperature	250 mL
1¾ cups	sugar	425 mL
7	eggs, separated	7
1 tsp.	vanilla	5 mL
4 tbsp.	grated orange rind	60 mL
2 cups	sifted cake flour	500 mL
½ cup	farina (Cream of Wheat)	125 mL
⅓ cup	slivered almonds	75 mL
2 tsp.	baking powder	10 mL
2 cups	water	500 mL
1 tsp.	lemon juice	5 mL
3	cinnamon sticks	3
10	whole cloves	10
3 tbsp.	Grand Marnier	45 mL

Preheat oven to 350°F (180°C).

In a large mixing bowl, beat the butter with ½ cup (125 mL) of sugar until light and fluffy. Beat in the egg yolks 1 at a time. Add the vanilla and orange rind. Stir in the flour, farina and almonds.

Beat the egg whites until stiff. Gradually beat in ½ cup (125 mL) of the sugar, until meringue is very stiff. Fold into the batter along with the baking powder.

Turn the batter into a greased 10 x 14" (25 x 35 cm) baking pan. Bake for 35-40 minutes, or until tester comes out clean.

Cool to room temperature in the pan.

Make the syrup by combining water, lemon juice, remaining ¾ cup (175 mL) sugar, cinnamon sticks and cloves in a small saucepan. Place over medium heat. Bring to a boil and boil for 5 minutes. Strain and discard spices. Add Grand Marnier. Spoon a little of the syrup over each serving.

Torta de Aceite a la Gallega

Galician Cake

1 cup	all-purpose flour	250 mL
1 tsp.	baking powder	5 mL
½ cup	sugar	125 mL
⅓ cup	olive oil	75 mL
3	medium eggs, separated	3
1 tsp.	grated lemon rind	5 mL
1	lemon, juice of	1

Set oven at 350°F (180°C).

Sift flour and baking powder into a mixing bowl. Stir in the sugar. Make a well in the center and pour in the oil, egg yolks, lemon rind and lemon juice. Blend together well.

Beat egg whites until stiff. Fold into the batter. Pour batter into a buttered 4 x 8" (1.5 L) loaf pan.

Bake for 45 minutes, check with cake tester. Turn cake out onto rack and cool.

Clafouti aux Framboises et Bluets

Raspberry and Blueberry Cake

France

Serves 8

This cake resembles a torte.

3 tbsp.	butter, at room temperature	45 mL
3	eggs	3
¼ cup	sugar	60 mL
¼ cup	milk	60 mL
1 cup	sifted flour	250 mL
¼ tsp.	allspice	1 mL
⅓ cup	chopped almonds	75 mL
1 cup	fresh or frozen raspberries (if frozen, thaw)	250 mL
1 cup	fresh or frozen blueberries (if frozen, thaw)	250 mL
4 tbsp.	icing sugar	60 mL
2 tbsp.	Kirsch, cognac or 1 tsp. (5 mL) vanilla	30 mL

Heat oven to 400°F (200°C).

Use the butter to grease a fluted 10" (25 cm) bundt pan, baking dish or cake pan.

Beat eggs and sugar until smooth and fluffy. Heat milk until very hot in a small saucepan. Gradually blend the flour into the egg mixture, alternating with a little of the milk to make a batter.

Blend in remainder of milk, add the allspice and almonds.

Pour a thin layer of the batter into the buttered pan. Bake for 5 minutes only, to set the batter.

Add the berries to the batter in the saucepan, stir gently only to coat berries. Pour over the baked batter.

Sprinkle 3 tbsp. (45 mL) of icing sugar over top.

Bake for 15 minutes then lower heat to 375°F (190°C). Bake for a further 30 minutes, or until center is firm and tester comes out clean.

Drizzle with Kirsch and sprinkle remainder of icing sugar over cake.

Serve warm.

OPTIONAL:
Top each serving with whipped cream.

Brazo De Gitano

Gypsy Roll

A classic Spanish cake, it is similar to a jelly roll.

CUSTARD FILLING

⅔ cup	milk	150 mL
½ tsp.	vanilla	2 mL
2 tbsp.	rum or strong black coffee	30 mL
2	egg yolks	2
¼ cup	sugar	60 mL
2 tbsp.	cornstarch	30 mL

CAKE

4	eggs	4
½ cup	sugar	125 mL
1 cup	sifted self-rising flour	250 mL
¼ tsp.	salt	1 mL
¼ cup	icing sugar	60 mL

Place milk, vanilla, rum or coffee in a small saucepan. Bring slowly to a boil, then remove from heat, allow to cool slightly. In small bowl, beat together the egg yolks, sugar and cornstarch. Whisk the egg mixture into the milk and cook over medium heat for 5 minutes, stirring constantly, until thick and smooth. Allow to cool before using.

Heat oven to 400°F (200°C).

Butter a jelly roll pan 10 x 14" (25 x 35 cm) and dust thoroughly with flour. In large mixing bowl, whisk the eggs and sugar together until mixture is pale. Add flour and salt to the egg mixture and fold in carefully. Pour into the pan, tilting the pan from side to side to spread the mixture evenly. Bake for 12-15 minutes, or until golden brown and springy to the touch.

Sprinkle the icing sugar on a sheet of waxed paper a little longer than the jelly roll pan.

Turn warm sponge cake over onto the sugar.

Spread cake with the custard filling then carefully roll up lengthwise.

Wrap in waxed paper to store. Chill before serving. Dust with icing sugar again and cut into slices.

INDEX

Share *A Taste of the Mediterranean* with a friend

Order *A Taste of the Mediterranean* and *A Taste of Lebanon* at $21.95 per book plus $4.00 (total order) for shipping and handling.

A Taste of Lebanon _____ x $21.95 = $ _____
A Taste of the Mediterranean _____ x $21.95 = $ _____
Postage and handling_____ = $ _____4.00_____
Subtotal _____ = $ _____
In Canada add 7% GST OR 15% HST where applicable_____ = $ _____
Total enclosed _____ = $ _____

U.S. and international orders payable in U.S. funds./ Price is subject to change.

NAME: _____
STREET: _____
CITY: _____ PROV./STATE _____
COUNTRY _____ POSTAL CODE/ZIP _____

Please make cheque or money order payable to: **A Taste of Lebanon Enterprises**
  (no C.O.D. orders)   **Box 6110 Station "A"**
                                           Calgary, Alberta
                                           Canada   T2H 2L4

For fund raising or volume purchases, contact **A Taste of Lebanon Enterprises** for volume rates.

Please allow 3-4 weeks for delivery

Share *A Taste of the Mediterranean* with a friend

Order *A Taste of the Mediterranean* and *A Taste of Lebanon* at $21.95 per book plus $4.00 (total order) for shipping and handling.

A Taste of Lebanon _____ x $21.95 = $ _____
A Taste of the Mediterranean _____ x $21.95 = $ _____
Postage and handling_____ = $ _____4.00_____
Subtotal _____ = $ _____
In Canada add 7% GST OR 15% HST where applicable_____ = $ _____
Total enclosed _____ = $ _____

U.S. and international orders payable in U.S. funds./ Price is subject to change.

NAME: _____
STREET: _____
CITY: _____ PROV./STATE _____
COUNTRY _____ POSTAL CODE/ZIP _____

Please make cheque or money order payable to: **A Taste of Lebanon Enterprises**
  (no C.O.D. orders)   **Box 6110 Station "A"**
                                           Calgary, Alberta
                                           Canada   T2H 2L4

For fund raising or volume purchases, contact **A Taste of Lebanon Enterprises** for volume rates.

Please allow 3-4 weeks for delivery

Mary Salloum, invites you to enjoy the authentic flavors of the Middle East. As marketing manager for a Calgary Bakery, Mary introduced pita bread throughout Western Canada. During her cooking demonstrations she was besieged for her recipes. Another motivation in writing this book was the desire to pass on her Lebanese culinary heritage to her Canadian-born children, son Danny and daughter Dana. Now, as owner of several Calgary Lebanese restaurants, Mary is enticing Calgarians with the tantalizing dishes of the Mediterranean. *A Taste of Lebanon* is a cultural as well as a gastronomic delight. It is an excellent guide to the incredible diversity of Lebanese cuisine. Mary's recipes are a marriage of the opulent, mysterious east with the practical west. While maintaining the genuine flavors of the Middle East, Mary Salloum has adapted her recipes to suit western lifestyles and kitchens. *A Taste of Lebanon* is a valuable resource for the student of Lebanese cookery and a gourmet delight for those who desire a taste of the exotic. Her second book, *A Taste of the Mediterranean* presents a culinary and cultural tour of the Mediterranean.